# *The* MINIATURE SCHNAUZER

EDITED BY
JUDY CHILDERLEY

BEST of BREED

## ACKNOWLEDGEMENTS

The publishers would like to thank the following for help with photography: Judy Childerley (Childgait); Caroline Waring (Caskayd): David Webb (Mantricks); Kirsty Sanders (Zakmayo); Liz Longdin (Wellingley); Maxine, Nancy and Arthur Silsby; Katherine Browning and Scruffy; Pets As Therapy.

Cover photo: © Tracy Morgan Animal Photography (www.animalphotographer.co.uk)
Dog featured is Childgait Cotswold Bling ('Moe'), sired by Ch. Risepark Mister Right

The British Breed Standard reproduced in Chapter 7 is the copyright of the Kennel Club and published with the club's kind permission. Extracts from the American Breed Standard are reproduced by kind permission of the American Kennel Club.

## THE QUESTION OF GENDER
**The 'he' pronoun is used throughout this book instead of the rather impersonal 'it',
but no gender bias is intended.**

First published in 2011 by The Pet Book Publishing Company Limited
Chepstow, NP16 7LG, UK
Reprinted in 2013
© 2011 Pet Book Publishing Company Limited.

**ISBN**
978-1-906305-51-2
1-906305-51-X

Printed and bound in China through Printworks Int. Ltd.

# CONTENTS

# GETTING TO KNOW MINIATURE SCHNAUZERS

# Chapter 1

If there is one word to sum up the Miniature Schnauzer, it is 'adaptable'. In terms of size and temperament, this is a dog that will fit in with any lifestyle – he will be an outstanding companion to a single person or a couple, regardless of age and occupation, and he will be just as happy being in the hub of family life. Town or country, apartment or mansion – a Miniature Schnauzer will love his home and will enjoy life to the full. There is one consideration that all prospective owners should bear in mind: a Miniature Schnauzer is a 'people dog', and he will not thrive if he is left to spend long periods on his own.

## PHYSICAL CHARACTERISTICS
The Miniature Schnauzer is a most distinctive-looking breed with his muscular, compact body, his long head, his beard and busy eyebrows – and those dark eyes that are always sparking and full of fun.

Bred down from his larger cousin, the Standard Schnauzer, the Miniature measures around 36 cms (14 ins) at the shoulder and weighs around 8 kgs (17.5 lbs); bitches are slightly smaller. This is a perfect size for a dog – not too big and not too small; he is sufficiently robust to enjoy the rigours of family life, but is not too much of handful for older owners.

The head is the hallmark of the breed. It is strong and flat between the ears, with a powerful, blunt muzzle. The ears are high-set, and the arched eyebrows frame the medium-sized, oval eyes. The expression is often described as "keen" – and that is entirely typical of a Miniature Schnauzer when something has caught his attention. But he also has a 'twinkle' in his eye, seeming to say he can't wait for the next bit of fun to come his way!

The Miniature Schnauzer has a double coat: a harsh, wiry topcoat to protect him from the elements and a soft, dense undercoat to keep him warm. Like many of the terrier breeds, the Miniature Schnauzer does not shed his coat – or shedding is so minimal as to be almost unnoticeable. This is a bonus for allergy sufferers, but it does mean your dog will need regular trips to the grooming parlour to have his coat clipped. This does not apply to show dogs, who have their coats carefully hand-stripped to maintain the correct texture. In fact, show presentation of the Miniature Schnauzer is art in itself – but if you use an experienced groomer, a pet can still look very smart and typical of the breed.

# THE COLOURS

**Pepper and salt.**

**Black and silver.**

**Black.**

**White.**

## THE COLOURS

There are four colours that are recognised:

- Pepper and salt: The topcoat is made up of black and white banded hairs, and solid black and white unbanded hairs, with the banded hairs predominating. This colour can vary in shades from light to dark. The eyebrows, whiskers, cheeks and leg furnishings are light or silver grey.
- Black: The topcoat is a rich, glossy solid colour, with the undercoat a less intense shade of black.
- Black and silver: Dogs of this colour are solid black with silver markings on the eyebrows, muzzle, chest, legs, and under the tail.
- White: This colour has been recognised in Europe, but it has only recently been accepted in the UK. It is not recognised in the US.

# TOPS AND TAILS

In the UK – and most other countries excluding North America – Miniature Schnauzers have V-shaped ears that naturally fold forwards. In North America, ears may be cropped and, in this case, they point straight upwards coming to a sharp point.

As the breed was originally conceived, the tail was set on high and docked to three joints. Docking is now illegal throughout Europe, and we are now becoming used to seeing full tails. The tail is thick at the root and tapering towards the top; it is carried as straight as possible and the instruction in the Breed Standard is that it should be "carried jauntily", which matches the personality of the breed. As breeding with full tails becomes established, the type of tail and tail carriage will become more uniform. In North America, docking is still permitted, and the short tail is carried high.

**Cropped ears.**

**Docked tail.**

**V-shaped folded ears.**

**Full tail.**

The Miniature Schnauzer loves nothing more than to be with his beloved family.

## TEMPERAMENT

The Miniature Schnauzer has a matchless temperament – and that is the great appeal of the breed. He is friendly, outgoing and interested in everything that is going on. He is described as "alert" in the Breed Standard, and this is exactly how he behaves. If he hears the slightest noise or catches sight of something new, he is off to investigate – giving a series of barks to tell you what he is doing.

The Standard Schnauzer was originally used as a watch dog, guarding the stable yard and keeping the rat population at bay. The Miniature Schnauzer, which inherits many of the Standard Schnauzer's characteristics, is placed in the Terrier Group in the USA – but he is not recognised as a terrier in the UK. The original, British-bred terriers were used to go to earth and bolt vermin; the Schnauzer did not perform this function, and has little true terrier blood in its lines.

This is relevant when analysing the typical Miniature Schnauzer temperament. This breed has all the characteristics of an alert watch dog but he does not have the feisty nature of some small terrier breeds.

The Miniature Schnauzer is described as "reliable" – and although this does not sound like an outstanding virtue – it should be considered as one. You want a dog with a temperament you can depend on, a dog you can trust with family – including small children – with friends, and even with strangers. Any self-respecting Mini will be vocal in his greeting, but he will soon settle down and enjoy being given some extra attention.

This is a breed that relates to people, and Miniature Schnauzers have an amazing knack of fitting into their owners' lifestyles. They are so keen to be part of everything that is going on that they somehow make themselves indispensible. The companionship you will enjoy from a Miniature Schnauzer is second to none – but, like all good things, it does not come for free. This is a breed that *needs* company; he will be deeply miserable – and possibly destructive – if he is left for lengthy periods.

## LIVING IN A FAMILY

The Miniature Schnauzer will be happy if he is the much-loved dog of a single person, he will be the perfect dog for a couple, and he will thrive if he is part of a family with children. He will adapt to all these roles with equal enthusiasm and will delight his owners with his own special sense of fun.

If you have young children, it is important that they learn to respect the dog. A Miniature Schnauzer is extremely tolerant, but no dog should put up with being pulled or poked or teased with food or toys. However, if you get the ground rules established, your Miniature Schnauzer will soon become an integral part of family life.

## LIVING WITH OTHER DOGS

We are fortunate that the Miniature Schnauzer is a very sociable dog. He loves his human family first and foremost, but he will enjoy canine company. Miniature Schnauzers are very collectable, and many owners end up with a Mini gang who all live together in complete harmony. If you do go in for collecting Miniature Schnauzers, make sure each one gets some individual attention, so they have some time when they feel extra special.

The Miniature Schnauzer is generally self-assured and confident, and he will mix well with different breeds, regardless of their size.

## BE WARNED!

The Miniature Schnauzer is a vocal breed, and he believes his most important job in life is to give you warning of strangers or visitors approaching. You will be amazed at his sense of hearing – he will start barking long before you have sensed that there is anyone in the vicinity.

This is a great asset in that you have an excellent watch dog who sounds the alarm, but it is not followed up by any feeling of suspicion or aggression once people are allowed in your house.

Be aware that if you keep more than one Miniature Schnauzer, they do tend to set each other off, so make sure you teach them that they are allowed to bark a warning, but they must be quiet when you tell them.

*For more information, see Chapter Six: Training and Socialisation.*

## TRAINABILITY

There is no doubting the Miniature Schnauzer's intelligence – you only have to see his alert expression and quick reactions to appreciate that this is a dog who lives on his wits. He is easy to train because he 'gets' what you want, but he is equally capable of running circles around you if you let him!

Most Miniature Schnauzers have a low threshold of boredom and will quickly tire of monotonous training exercises. You need to be creative and keep training fresh and interesting. The Miniature Schnauzer loves to perform, so why not teach him some tricks to show off when visitors come round?

A lot of Miniature Schnauzers adopt a 'job', such as fetching the mail or going to find your slippers. They enjoy having something to do, and they are particularly keen on getting a treat to reward their efforts!

In the USA, a wide variety of breeds try obedience trials with a fair degree of success. In the UK, the sport is dominated by breeds such as Border Collies and German Shepherd Dogs, but the Mini is certainly bright enough to have a go. He also makes a great agility dog, where his quick wits – and equally fast reactions – are an asset.

**Beware! Miniature Schnauzers are very collectable.**

# A VERY SPECIAL SCHNAUZER

I t is widely recognised that interacting with animals has great therapeutic value, and dogs are now welcomed into many institutions, such as care homes, schools, prisons and hospital. Working with their owners, therapy dogs – known as Pets As Therapy (PAT) Dogs in the UK – bring comfort to those who are deprived of the company of pets. The Miniature Schnauzer is perfect for this role because of his friendly nature and his handy size.

**Katherine Browning with therapy dog Scruffy**

*Katherine Browning, from Cheltenham, Gloucestershire, first got involved in therapy work when her Miniature Schnauzer, Scruffy, was just over two years old. They are now regular visitors at an adult day care centre, and also at a psychiatric hospital. Recently, Katherine and Scruffy were nominated for the Unsung Heroes awards, which recognises outstanding achievements and contributions made by volunteers working in the community.*

"I was always more of a cat person and I didn't really consider owning a dog until I went on a trip to America," said Katherine. "I stayed with friends and – much to my surprise – I found myself asking if I could take their dog out for walks, and I really enjoyed the experience.

"When I returned home, I found my parents increasingly needed my help and support. I was having to travel some distance to see them, and then spend time sorting things out for them. I decided that a dog would give me companionship on the journeys and would also give me the excuse to go out for walks and have a little 'me time' to recharge the batteries.

"I had never owned a dog before, so I drew up a long list of what I wanted from my chosen breed. I wanted a dog that was good with children and old people, who was trainable and could adapt to different environments. I wanted a real, robust dog – but I also needed him to be a handy, portable size. The answer was a Miniature Schnauzer, and since getting Scruffy, I have never looked back.

"I could never believe a dog could be so loving and so much a part of my everyday life. Scruffy was a very lively puppy, but now he is the perfect dog – chilled and relaxed at home, and keen as mustard when it is time to go out for his daily walks.

"I work in training and assessment, and I first found out about PAT dogs when I picked up a leaflet in a women's prison where I working. I applied for more details and decided it was something I would like to do. Each dog has to be individually assessed before they become a fully qualified PAT dog, and I was so nervous when it was our turn to be examined. In fact, Scruffy had no problems at all – he is so loving and friendly – he was more than happy to be handled by a stranger and to show he could take a treat gently! He is pretty much bombproof, so he was not worried about being exposed to a sudden loud noise. His lead walking did not get the best marks – but we're working on that!

"Our first visit was to an adult day care centre – and, as it turned out, we were due to go a few days after my father died. I was dreading it, and thought maybe I should cancel. But I decided to go ahead – and it was the best thing I could have done. Scruffy was wonderful, and I got such a kick from seeing what a difference he was making. It was incredibly therapeutic for me, as well as for the people we were visiting.

"When we were more established as a team, I agreed to become a visitor at the local psychiatric hospital. Some people find this quite disturbing and it can be pretty challenging, but I felt it was a place where Scruffy and I could make a contribution. I find that it is important to work closely with the staff and then you can give help where it is most needed.

"There was one memorable occasion when an occupational therapist asked me to take Scruffy to see one of the patients who had become almost entirely silent and uncommunicative. She just sat perfectly still, staring at nothing. I went and sat next to her, and sat Scruffy on my lap. I introduced myself and started talking to her, and, to begin with, there was no response. Then, very slowly, she lifted her hand and reached out for Scruffy. He was such a good boy, he sat still and she gave him a few gentle strokes. After while, I said it was time for me to go, and I would come and see her again on my next visit. Just as I was getting up, she reached out and grasped my hand. The member of staff who had called me over could not believe it – and I must admit, we both had a bit of a cry. It was so moving to see her respond.

"As well as attending the hospital, we accompany some of the patients on organised walks, which we all very much enjoy. For me, it is all about treating people with the respect they deserve, and I hope that Scruffy and I are able to make a small difference in their lives."

**Scruffy: A true ambassador for the breed.**

# THE FIRST MINIATURE SCHNAUZERS

## Chapter 2

If you own a purebred dog, it is always interesting to understand something of the breed's origins. As well as appreciating some of the Miniature Schnauzers and kennels that have influenced and shaped the breed's development, some could well be in the pedigree of your own special Miniature.

Unlike most breeds, Schnauzers were not bred just for their looks or an ability to do a specific job. They were appreciated for their splendid adaptability and ruggedness, as well as for the fact they could think for themselves – qualities that make all three sizes stand out when compared to other breeds. Each size was bred for a different reason, which is reflected in their character and temperament.

## SCHNAUZER ORIGINS

There are three varieties of Schnauzer: Giant, Standard and Miniature, in descending order of size. The Standard, as we call the middle-sized Schnauzer, is the original of the family. Renowned as a versatile general farm and drover's dog, as well as an excellent catcher of rats and other vermin, the Standard was also valued as an extra hand because of his versatility and ability to think, which made for a strong one-dog/one-master relationship. This is a trait still carried through to today's dogs.

Trends and fashions change, and, in the 19th century, small dogs were being accepted in the home, becoming part of the family. However, they still needed to make a contribution. Miniatures were not only congenial but were also excellent watchdogs, albeit somewhat vocal. Today, the Miniature Schnauzer is extremely sociable and adapts easily to his owner's lifestyle, whatever that may be.

Giant Schnauzers came along in the early 20th century when Germany was developing the police dog. Breeders crossed black Great Danes with Standard Schnauzers to produce a sensible, thinking, big dog that was affable and protective, but one that would also be a deterrent, barking a warning rather than being overtly aggressive.

The Standard Schnauzer's homeland is Bavaria – southern Germany of today – an alpine area with high and low pastures. It has harsh winters, making soundness in body and limbs essential for a dog, along with the need for a harsh, tight-fitting coat that would insulate and be water-resistant. It is interesting to reflect on how important and essential those qualities would have been in the early years. So much so that when

**The Standard Schnauzer: The medium-sized 'original' variety of the Schnauzer family.** *Photo: Tracy Morgan.*

**The Giant Schnauzer was bred to be a big, thinking dog, with protective instincts.** *Photo © istockphoto.com/Susan H. Smith.*

**The Miniature Schnauzer: Now the most popular of the three varieties.**

the first Breed Standard was drawn up in 1880 and judging was on the points system, coat carried five more points that other requirements.

In Stuttgart there is a statue, dated 1620, of the Night Watchman and his Dog, clearly showing a dog of Schnauzer type. Coincidentally, the first special show for Schnauzers also took place in Stuttgart, over 200 years later in 1890.

## DEVELOPMENT OF THE MINIATURE

It is generally accepted that Miniature Schnauzers were not developed by using runts, but were carefully and intentionally bantamised in size using small dogs, including the Affenpinscher, the small Spitz and the rough-coated German Terrier with the Schnauzer. Appreciating this and taking into account the Breed Standard, we can understand the intention was to produce a miniature of the Standard – a small, sturdy and sound working dog having nothing terrier- or toy-like about him, but also having the character and admired qualities of the Standard Schnauzer.

When Miniatures first came to Britain in 1928, then known as Affenschnauzers, they were registered along with Standard Schnauzers and not given a separate register until 1932. The Charles Crufts show the following year was the first to give the breed separate classes. Kennel Club Challenge Certificates were first granted in

# NAMING THE BREED

The Schnauzer is not only unique for its pepper and salt colour of light through to dark shades of grey banded hairs, but it is also the only breed to take its name from one of its kind. The winner of the rough-haired Pinscher class at a dog show in Hanover in 1879 was named Schnauzer, which, loosely translated, means beard or snout. When the first Breed Standard was drawn up, they were referred to as German Rough Haired Terriers or ratting dogs, as well as Schnauzers.

1935 at the West of England Ladies Society show at Cheltenham. To become a Champion three certificates are required, under three different judges, with one to be won over the age of a year. Shortly after, the breed had a name change to Miniature Schnauzer as a result of an objection by the German breed club.

In Britain a breed club had been formed in 1933, but for reasons that have never been clear, was dissolved in 1936. Thereafter – probably because of their small numbers – breeders were content to be under the umbrella of the Schnauzer Club of Great Britain (founded in 1928) and the parent club for Standards. The club still supports Miniatures today, as well as Giants from when they

were first imported. Both breeds subsequently formed their own clubs.

Today's Miniature Schnauzer Club was formed in 1953, 25 years after the breed had first been introduced to the country.

Looking at the progress and development of Miniatures in Britain, it is significant to note the influence of American bloodlines. Although Germany and Europe are geographically closer, the links with America and its breeders have been much the stronger, particularly through influential breeders and bloodlines on both sides of the Atlantic. The pluses from the American influence can be seen in the early breeding, as well as the ongoing improvements, particularly in type and temperament.

## EARLY CHAMPIONS

When we look back to the earliest years of the breed in Britain, the pepper and salt dog, Ch. Enstone Cito, was the first Champion made up in 1936. The following year, Ch. Enstone Beda became the first black title maker; we had to wait until 1986 for the first black and silver Champion. In all, three dogs and four bitches became Champions before the outbreak of war in 1939. For the duration of the war, Championship shows were suspended and showing was restricted by a distance of 25 miles due to petrol restrictions. They were held in support of the Red Cross or the war effort.

The German breeding of Heinzelmannchen proved an interesting link between the earliest years and when interest in breeding and showing began to grow after the war years. In 1936 the two German-bred Crowsteps half-sisters, Hilvaria and Grafin, both Heinzelmannchen-bred, were the breed's second and third title makers. In the early fifties, Donald Becker (Dondeau) imported the cropped Dondeau Favorite Heinzelmannchen, who sired three Champions.

## FORMATIVE YEARS

The Fifties to the mid-Sixties were the formative years for the breed in Britain, due principally to two breeders: Donald Becker

and Mrs Doreen Crowe (Deltone). Donald Becker was the main breeder and exhibitor in these formative years with 13 Champions carrying the Dondeau affix in the first seven years of Championship shows that were held after the war. His Ch. Dondeau Hamerica, born in 1945, and a son of the first post-war American import, Minquas Harriet, proved to be an influential sire, as Mrs Crowe based her breeding programme on the two Hamerica half-sisters, Ch. Dondeau Hiya Deltone and Ch. Dondeau Harvest Moon. Mrs Crowe's handler, Billy Norman, trimmed and smartened the breed, giving it shape and style.

The American-bred Ch.

Ch. Eastwright Sea-Fantasy (right) and Ch. Rownhams Batman. *Photo: Joy Warren.*

Rannoch Dune Randolph of Appeline sired Ch. Deltone Appeline Doughboy out of a Hamerica grand-daughter, and he brought the breed to notice by his many show successes. He, and his progeny, set the look, style and sturdiness of the breed in Britain.

Between 1950 and 1972 the Deltone affix was associated with 18 Champions and a further 27 English Champions had either a Deltone sire or dam, several becoming significant sires or dams in their own right. The influence of Deltones – and particularly Doughboy – which provided such a sound foundation for the breed, should never be undervalued or forgotten.

## INFLUENTIAL BREEDERS

Two kennels with their roots in the late Fifties, both starting with a Deltone bitch, are Miss Pamela Morrison-Bell (Eastwight) and Peter Newman (Risepark), both to become influential in different ways. Miss Morrison-Bell and her successful line of Eastwights stayed mainly within their own breeding. The Riseparks of Peter Newman – from 1985 in partnership with Barry Day – represent the top-winning kennel and are highly respected for the influence of their American imports.

### EASTWIGHT

Always enthusiastic for the black and silver colour, Miss Morrison-Bell's most notable dog in the colour was Canadian Ch. Eastwight Sea Voyager.

Born in 1967, he proved an influence on the colour in North America and in Europe. It is also fitting that the final Eastwight titleholder, Ch. Eastwight Sea Mannikin, was a black and silver, made up in 1993 – the first and only title maker in the colour for his breeder.

Over the years, Eastwight enjoyed considerable and consistent show successes but, by a quirk of fate, Best of Breed at Crufts proved elusive. The first Champion for the kennel was Ch. Eastwight Sea Nymph, made up in 1960. She was sired by Rownhams Cavalier, who was owned and bred by Elaine Quigley, an equally enthusiastic supporter of the black and silvers. In all, there have been 20 homebred Eastwight Champions, as well as two not homebred, plus two jointly owned with Elaine Quigley. The roll of honour includes a female line of descendancy of five Champions, an achievement Miss Morrison-Bell always felt proud of. The well-named Ch. Rimmick Ringmaster co-owned by Janet Callow (Buffels) and Betty Fletcher (Arbey), with his strong Eastwight-Rownhams breeding, sired 11 Champions, proving a notable advertisement for his bloodlines. He enjoyed a most successful show career, and was the breed's joint third leading sire and the highest placed non-imported dog.

### RISEPARK

Peter Newman and Barry Day's Risepark holds an unequalled position in the breed through

**Ch. Irrenhaus Aims To Please at Rispeark (Am. Ch. Regency's Right On Target – Am. Ch. Irrenhuas Flight Pattern).**
*Photo: Sally Anne Thompson.*

Miniatures imported and their influence in Britain. This has been gained through long-standing friendships, a shared love for the breed, and confidence in the Miniatures chosen. Added to this, each import, in turn, has complemented earlier imports and their breeding, which has had a major influence not only on the Risepark dogs but on the breed as a whole.

The most influential Miniature Schnauzer has been Ch. Awesomes in the Mood with Risepark (Moodie), a son of American Ch. Rampages Representative who is acknowledged as one of America's all-time greats and outstanding sires. Moodie's offspring have an

instantly recognisable look and style, and his 14 Champion offspring make him the breed's second top-producing sire. A well-appreciated stud, his influence is very much across the breed and continues to be seen in succeeding generations.

Ch. Irrenhaus Impact at Risepark, linebred on Am. Ch. Skyline Blue Spruce, was imported 20 years before Moodie and was made a Champion in 1982. He, too, proved to be an important sire and with 11 Champion offspring is joint third in the stud listing. Blue Sprice was recognised for his excellent Schnauzer type and qualities, which are still highly sought after today. Along with Am. Ch. Regencys Right on

Target, he is considered to be a model for the breed.

Blue Spruce's background is shared with the breed's most influential import and sire, Ch. Travelmors US Mail, who is a Blue Spruce son. The common link of blood, type and quality with the Miniatures being bred, shown and recognised represented a golden period for the entire breed and gave a stability of type, as had Doughboy and the Deltone breeding earlier.

Despite the restrictions of quarantine, there has always been an international element to breeding and showing in Britain. Ch. Jidjis Min Cato at Risepark was Swedish-bred, but with an American sire and an English-bred mother. Imported in 1975, he proved a popular stud whose influence on type, temperament and sturdiness was clearly seen. He is joint sixth in the stud hierarchy with eight Champions.

Back in the sixties, Risepark also had a hand in Roundway Anklet being the breed's top brood with six Champions, three being by Risepark Northern Cockade and three by Ch. Risepark Bon-Ell Taurus, the first American import to come to Risepark in 1968. When Ch. Lonestars Earmarked by Chattelane won his Championship in 2009, he was

**Ch. Travelmors US Mail: A highly influential stud dog.**

the 58th Miniature Champion for Risepark and their sixth imported male.

## ICCABOD

Although no longer active, the value and influence of the Iccabod Miniature Schnauzers of the late Pam Radford and Dorrie Clarke has been reflected across the breed. Always highly regarded breeders and exhibitors, they were prominent in the Seventies and Eighties, helped by the all-breed successes of several of their dogs. Most notable were their two cleverly-named American imports: the bitch, Ch. Travelmors from US to You, the first of her sex in the breed to go Best in Show at a General Championship Show, and the dog, Ch. Travelmors US Mail, a delightful character, successful as a show dog and outstanding as a sire. With 17 Champions to his

credit, he is the breed's top stud; his qualities are seen in, and carried, by many of today's outstanding dogs and bitches. All of this is no surprise, as he is a son of Am. Ch. Skylines Blue Spruce.

Ch. Iccabod Chervil and his son, Ch. Iccabod Mixed Herbs, who is out of the American bitch Ch. Travelmors From US to You, both sired eight Champions, all very much of a pattern – a blending of earlier American bloodlines with the new. Their names recall some impressive Miniatures, as well as how strong the breed was in their day – not just in the hands of a few breeders, but seen across the breed.

## BEAULEA

A kennel that notably reflects the Iccabod look are the Miniatures of Pat and Ray Franklin with their Beauleas. They all stem from Iccabod Jaywalker, a daughter of From US to You and litter sister to Ch. Iccabod Mixed Herbs, which gave them a sound and solid foundation for their own breeding programme. They have consistently held on to their strong bitch line, a policy that has enabled them to establish an instantly recognisable line of Champion dogs and bitches.

## MALENDA

Glenys and Don Allen's Malenda Miniature Schnauzers also have a look that is instantly recognisable. Their breeding has been respected and very successful since Ch. Malenda Masquerade was made up back in 1975. It has always been a small hobby kennel where only bitches are kept and the pepper and salt colour bred. The successes and reputation of the Malenda Miniatures shows just how consistently successful a small kennel can be, through knowledge of the breed and giving careful consideration to each mating.

**Ch. Beaulea Sweet Sensation: This bitch became a Champion at 15 months.**

## DEANSGATE

Pam McLaren and Elizabeth Cooke with the Deansgate Miniatures will always be associated with Ch. Luke Lively at Deansgate, the breed record holder with 40 Challenge Certificates. Born in 1983, Luke's showing days covered some eight years, and are particularly remembered for his successes at club shows as a veteran.

The partners have made up 15 Champions in Britain, and over the years a good number of Deansgate Miniatures have gone abroad and gained their titles. Deansgate Tom Bowler became a Champion in Sweden at the age

of 10, as well as earning other national titles – all from the veteran class. His wins at the Berlin Show, not once but twice, particularly pleased the partners, as it epitomises much of what they have been proud of over the years – producing quality that lasts in the show ring.

## CASTILLA

Fred and the late Phyl Morley were successful breeders and exhibitors. Their cleverly-named Ch. Castilla LinaJudo (translates as blueblood) had an outstanding show career that began as an exceptional puppy and brought Miniature Schnauzers to the notice of the general public, most noticeably by his Reserve Best in Show at Crufts in 1980. In the same year he also won the prestigious Contest of Champions. He was the breed's

leader with 31 Challenge Certificates before being overtaken by Luke.

## ARBEY

This well-known and well-regarded affix of Betty and Archie Fletcher all began with their first Miniature and first Champion, a bitch called Ch. Short and Sweet at Deansgate. She was a daughter of Ch. Buffels All American Boy at Deansgate and was made up in 1975. She became the foundation for breeding that has tended to stay within its own line to consistently produce Champions recognisable in type and style in both pepper and salt and black and silver colours.

## BUFFELS

This is the affix of Janet Callow, who, when she returned to Britain in the late Sixties after working in the well-known Travelmors kennels in America, brought with her the dog, Am. Ch. Travelmors Fantazio and the bitch, Riversedge Petite Pebbles. In 1969 she bred Buffels All American Boy, subsequently sold to the Deansgate partners who added their affix. He not only became Ch. Buffels All American Boy At Deansgate, gaining his title in 1971, but also went on to be one of the breed's early and important sires with nine Champions to his credit, from bitches with varied bloodlines. For some 20 years he was the breed's leading stud and today is in fifth place.

Having always admired the Eastwight and Rownhams Miniatures, Betty Fletcher and Janet Callow were pleased to be able to buy Rimmick Ringmaster as a 10-month-old puppy. With his Eastwight sire and Rownhams dam he proved an astute buy, not only for his success as a show dog – becoming a Champion in 1991– but also as an outstanding sire. With 11 Champions to his credit, he is equal third in the leading stud table and the highest placed non-imported dog. His first title maker was the much-admired Ch. Buffels Good Time Girl made up in 1992. He certainly suited the Arbeybuffles and Arbey breeding, making up as they do, the majority of his title makers. His influence is clearly seen in several other well-known kennels.

**Ch. Rimmick Ringmaster: A top sire for the breed.**
*Photo: Diane Pearce.*

## ARBEYBUFFELS
This affix came into being as a result of Betty Fletcher and Janet Callow becoming good friends and sharing so much in what they wanted for their Miniatures, and what they felt to be important for the breed.

The Ringmaster son, Ch.

Arbeybuffels This Guy Can, was the first title maker for the affix, made up in 1993, to be followed two years later by Ch. Arbeybuffels Go North. He was the partnership's first Champion in the black and silver colour, becoming so in four straight shows – a remarkable achievement for the colour – and with seven Challenge Certificates, he holds the record for black and silvers.

The partnership's Ch. Buffels Flashman is an interesting dog, being a son of the American-bred Jovials High Flyer of Sole Baye, imported by the Franklins (Beaulea) and out of the Australian-bred bitch Schonhardt Buffels Glory, who is strong in Hansenhaus American breeding. He has produced six Champions and his influence is seen outside

his home kennel. When the Flashman daughter, Ch. Arbeybuffels In The Mood, became a Champion in 2009 she was the 29th to do so for Arbey, Buffels and Arbeybuffles, all but three being homebred.

## ZAKMAYO
The Zakmayo Miniatures of Viv and Kirsty Sanders show just how the breed can captivate and charm. This mother and daughter partnership were involved with Dobermanns but thought they would like another breed and Miniatures caught their eye. Kirsty remarked that one small dog would not make much difference, little realising they would soon become hooked on the breed and one would quickly become several.

Their first Miniature was a Wendras-bred dog, and, by staying in the family, Ch. Wendras Dream Maker lived up to his name and became their first Champion in 1995. His son, Ch. Zakmayo Billy Whizz, the first home-bred title maker co-owned with Gail and Martin Wise and shown by Gail, proved a successful show dog and the top Miniature of 1996.

With a good eye and dedicated to the breed, Zakmayo has become a formidable name in

Miniature Schnauzer circles. The home-bred dogs and bitches that are being successfully shown, and their Champions, bear testament to this. Their American import, Ch. Tomar's Two Thumbs Up For Zakmayo, is the top Miniature and leading sire for 2009.

## CASKAYD

Caroline and Steve Wareing with the Caskayds came into Miniatures through Great Danes and Giant Schnauzers, having made up Champions in both. Their Giant, Ch. Jaffrak Keep Talking, holds the bitch breed record with 20 CCs. They found Miniatures delightful in so many ways, and only wish they had owned the breed a lot earlier.

Their first Miniature was the American import, Skansens Toyboy, who had actually come over to be a quarantine companion for a Giant Schnauzer that Frances Krall was importing. This was something Steve knew nothing about until he was taken to meet Caroline's Toyboy, just days before his release from quarantine.

Ch. Skansens Toyboy at Caskayd not only did exceedingly well as a show dog, and is the most winning black, but he also proved himself as a sire, and is

**Ch. Tomar's Two Thumbs Up To Zakmayo: Top Miniature 2009.**

behind today's most winning blacks. Although their foundation bitch, Jenmil Black Sequence, just missed out with becoming a Champion, she nevertheless proved herself a top producer with three Champions to her credit.

## JENMIL

Although it was a pepper and salt that brought Jennifer Milburn into the breed, it has been the blacks and black and silvers that have captured her interest. There have been good dogs bred in both colours. Ch. Jenmil Black Innovation and his son, Ch. Jenmil Black Inspiration, were benchmarks for the black colour, and her American black and silver import, Ward Creeks Silver Rocket, has proved a valuable addition for the black and silvers.

## LICHSTONE

This affix has been associated with Ann and Tony McDermott for some years now, but was first taken out by Stan Burke, Ann's father in the mid-Fifties, a time when the pepper and salt colour was the main interest for the breed. Now all three colours, including two pepper and salt Champions, carry the affix.

## DENBROUGH, ROCKSVILLE, ASHENCRUZ

Dennis and Joan Shaw with Denbrough and Rocksville, and their daughter Laura Burns with Ashencruz, breed and show all three colours, with no one colour preferred. When the black Ch. Rocksville Fatal Instinct won her title in 2001, she was the first home-bred black bitch to do so in over 30 years, and in 2003 when they won both CCs with home-bred blacks – this was a first for the colour.

The pepper and salt Ch. Ashencruz Allegiance to Denbrough proved an outstanding show dog with a career that began with winning his first certificate while still a puppy at the Schnauzer Club's Championship Show in 2008. He went on to win a total of 26 CCs, ending with a third time Best of Breed at the Utility Breeds Championship Show in 2008, and going on to Best in Show – a fitting finale. The top-winning Miniature in 2006 to 2008, he is also the top-winning Miniature with Group successes, winning four times, going second four times and fourth once, including a second and fourth placing with his two Best of Breed at Crufts.

## SUMMING UP

By looking at the dogs that have influenced the breed over the years, we can see that they are mainly American dogs, or those with American bloodlines, showing just how dominant the American influence has been on the breed in Britain. Little has been written about bitches, but that is the way it is. Bitches have much less opportunity to influence their breed, unlike a popular stud, and when they do, it is more usually through a dominant offspring who will pass on their special qualities, no matter the dog or bitch they are mated to.

Pam Radford and Dorri Clarkes' American-bred Ch. Travelmors From US To You illustrates this so well. Not only was she an outstanding bitch in the show ring, but she was also a remarkably influential brood through her two Champion sons, Ch. Iccabod Mixed Herbs (sired by Ch. Iccabod Chervil) and Ch.

Iccabod Travellers Tail (sired by their other import, Ch. Travelmors US Mail), who, between them, sired 14 Champions. At the other end of the scale, the qualities of the breed's top-producing bitch, Roundway Anklet, were to be passed on through just one of her offspring, Ch. Risepark Toreador.

The influence and strength of the bitches, and how the breeding of the successful kennels has been shaped and progressed, can be clearly seen with those bitches that have produced two or three Champions – something that also shows how the family influence has continued into succeeding generations. This is well illustrated by some of the Eastwight breeding of Miss Morrison-Bell. Her Ch. Eastwight Sea Fantasy was the dam of four Champions, three others each had three title makers, and her

foundation bitch (Deltone Delmanhatton) was the dam of two Champions.

The other side of the coin, but equally significant, is how some of the breed's outstanding winners in both sexes have failed to influence the breed as much as might have been expected. This highlights the uncertainties that come with breeding, as well as the fact that like does not always produce like.

Nowadays emphasis seems to be placed on the dog, especially if he is a top winner, with the qualities of the bitch and her influence on the litter seemingly very much underappreciated. In my experience, matings are very much a balancing act between what is good and wanted and what is unwanted, with both the sire and dam contributing.

## MINIATURE SCHNAUZERS IN THE US

*American breeder, exhibitor and judge of Miniature Schnauzers, Wyoma Clouss, has given us an overview of the breed's activity in the US.*

Ch. Dorem Display can be credited with the strongest influence on Miniature Schnauzers in the United States. As the breed's first 'super sire', he influences virtually every Miniature

**Ch. Travelmors From US To You: A Best in show winner and an important brood bitch.**

Schnauzer in the US show ring today. During his lifetime (1945-1959), he was our breed's first Best in Show winner, earning a total of five Bests in Show, and four Specialty Best of Breed wins. The sire of 42 Champions, Display's contribution carries on through his sons: Ch. Dorem Tribute (41 Champions), Ch. Delegate of Ledahof (5), Ch. Diplomat of Ledahof (29), and particularly, Ch. Meldon's Ruffian (26). Ruffian (1950-1965) became the breed's second multiple Best in Show winner, and has been the most influential of Display's sons. Ruffian's own descendants continue his winning tradition.

Am. Ch. Dorem Display: Breeder Dorothy Williams, Owner Audrey Meldon. He was the breed's first Best in Show winner, earning a total of five Bests in Show, and four Specialty Best of Breed awards.

*BLYTHEWOOD*
Starting in Miniature Schnauzers in 1949, Joan Huber's first home-bred Champion was Ch. Blythewood Merry Melody, whelped in 1956. Based in Pennsylvania, the Blythewood kennel name has become well known for quality Miniature Schnauzers around the world. Joan is also known as a top Miniature Schnauzer handler, piloting several dogs to the number-one spot. One example was her own Ch. Blythewood Chief Bosun in 1966. Joan also handled clients' dogs, including Ch. Mutiny Uproar in 1970, Ch. Sky Rocket's Bound to Win in 1973, Ch. Sibehil's Dark Shadows (black) in 1986 and 1987, and Ch. Enjoy's Phantom of the Opera (black and silver) who, in 1999, became the first black and silver to win the AMSC Montgomery County National Specialty.

Am. Ch. Meldon's Ruffian: Breeder Audrey Meldon, Owners Mr & Mrs George Hendrickson. He lived his life with professional handlers Larry and Alice Downey. Ruffian has been the most influential of the Display sons, with 26 Champions to his credit. He became the breed's second multiple Best in Show winner, and his descendants continue his winning tradition.

Am. Ch Blythewood National Acclaim: Breeder/Owner Joan Huber. Acclaim produced 32 Champions, won 17 Specialties lifetime, and a Best in Show in 1979.

Am.Ch. Blythewood Shooting Sparks: Breeder/Owner Joan Huber. Sparky produced 63 Champions, and won several Specialties, along with 10 Terrier Groups and a Best in Show.

Am. Ch. Penlan Paperboy. Breeders/Owners Lanny and Penny Hirstein. Paperboy won a Best in Show in 1973, and produced 44 Champions.
*Photo: Shafer.*

Am. Ch Penlan Peter Gunn: Breeders Lanny and Penny Hirstein, Owners Carol and Dr Carl Beiles. Peter Gunn was the Top Miniature Schnauzer in 1977 and won 15 Specialties, over 100 Best of Breed awards, with 60 Group placements. He also sired 73 Champions.                    *Photo: Graham.*

Ch Kelly's Pebwin's Hallelujah (black): Breeder/Owner Geri Kelly. Co-Owners Geri Kelly and Suzanne Steele. Hallelujah won three Best in Show with 23 Group Firsts, and was a top winner in 1990 & 1991.

Am. Ch. Playboy's Blockbuster. Breeder/Owner Carole Hansen Baws. Blockbuster was ranked as number 3 Miniature Schnauzer in 1974. He won two Specialties, 35 other Best of Breed awards with 21 Group placements. He sired 22 Champions.

Joan's top-producing Blythewood dogs include Ch. Blythewood His Majesty (11), Ch. Blythewood Main Gazebo (31), Ch. Blythewood National Anthem (25), Ch. Blythewood National Acclaim (32), Ch. Blythewood Ewok Von Der Stars (17), Ch. Blythewood On Camera (16), and the very special Ch. Blythewood Shooting Sparks, whelped in 1983, who produced 63 Champions. Blythewood provided the foundation for breeders such as Jilmar, Annfield, Attaway, Sathgate, Markworth, Jo-Mi, and many others.

## PENLAN

Lanny and Penny Hirstein purchased their first Miniature Schnauzer in 1961, and soon established Penlan as one of the most successful kennels over the next five decades. Based in Illinois, they also became well-known professional handlers. Top-producing Penlan dogs included Ch. Penlan Paragon (11 Champions) born in 1967, and his son, Ch. Penlan Paragon's Pride (30). Top-producing Paragon's Pride sons were: Ch. Penlan Pride's Promise (8), Ch. Merry Maker's Dyna-Mite (15), and Ch. Penlan Paperboy (44) born in 1971.

Pride's Promise sired Ch. Penlan Promissory (27), and Paperboy sired Ch. Valharra's Prize of Penlan (8), Ch. Charmar Copy Cat (24), and Ch. Richlene's Big Time (16). Ch. Penlan Checkmate (34), also born in 1971, sired Ch. Hi 'N' Mighty of Hansenhaus (7), Ch. Bardon Bounty Hunter (10), and Ch. Dardane Wagonmaster (9).

## KELLY

Starting in 1963, Geri Kelly is known for specialising in the colour black. Geri incorporated top pepper and salt sires such as Ch. Regency's Right On Target (78) and Ch. Penlan Peter Gunn (73) into her line of blacks to improve quality. In 1981, Am/Can./Berm. Ch. Kelly's K.E. Ebony Show Stopper was the first black to win an AMSC Specialty. Top bitch in 1982, Ch. Kelly's Flamboyant Black produced 10 Champions. Ch. Kelly's Magic Marker (black) (7) gave Gwen Mulheron of Daree a good start with two black Champions. Ch. Kelly's Pebwin's Hallelujah (black), was a top winner in both 1990 and 91, and a top sire, producing 35 Champions.

## HANSENHAUS

Carol Hansen Baws, Hansenhaus Miniature Schnauzers, has been known for such standout producers as Ch. Lanmark's Playboy (10), and his sons, Ch. Playboy's Special Edition (7), and Ch. Playboy's Blockbuster (22) who won two AMSC National Specialties. Blockbuster, born in 1972, sired Ch. Hi-Charge of Hansenhaus (11), Ch. Hundred Proof of Hansenhaus (7), and Ch. Baws Strait Shot V Hansenhaus (5) for Bob and Violet Baws, plus another six Champions for Shirley and Bob Rains of Rainbou. Ch. Hi-Charge of Hansenhaus produced 11 Champions. Other top-producing Hansenhaus dogs include Ch. Hi 'N' Mighty of Hansenhaus (7), Ch. JR Boomer of Hansenhaus, born in 1980,

(6), and Ch. Petty's EZ Goer of Hansenhaus (5). Carol's best-producing bitch has been Ch. Misbehaving of Hansenhaus (9).

More recently, Carol has been working with Pat and Kim Jacobs of Lion'L, producing Ch. Lion'L A-Train of Hansenhaus (6), among others.

## OUTSTANDING SIRES

In 1973, Ch. Penlan Checkmate sired one of the breed greats, a top winner as well as a top-producing sire, Ch. Penlan Peter Gunn (73). In turn, Peter Gunn sired Ch. Penlan Piston Packer (7), Ch. Carolane's Fancy That (7), Ch. Penlan Peter's Son (25), and Ch. Tomei Super Star (30). Ch. Penlan Pastatively (34) was whelped in 1995, sired by Ch. Robbie Soucy's Sunny Promise, out of Ch. Penlan Pastabilitites (5). Penlan provided the foundation for many other breeders, including Carolane, Richlene, Angler, Bardon, Valencia, Charmar, Tel-Mo, Maroch, Wyndwood, plus Karlshof and Galaxy, which are still active today.

In 1974, Carol Parker produced one of our most influential dogs, Ch. Skyline's Blue Spruce. The Top Miniature Schnauzer in 1976, Blue Spruce was a special dog who made a huge impact on today's Miniature Schnauzers. Blue Spruce sired 55 Champions, who were then top producers themselves, including Ch. Regency's Right On (34) who in 1980 sired Ch. Regency's Right On Target (78). In turn, Target's top-producing son was Ch.

Am. Ch. Skyline's Blue Spruce (as a puppy). Breeder/Owner Carol Parker. He won Best of Breed at Montgomery County in 1975, was Number One Miniature Schnauzer in 1976, and sired 55 Champions.
*Photo; Dan Kiedrowski.*

Eng. & Am. Ch. Repitition's Kiss (black & silver, natural ears): Breeder Kurt Garmaker, Owner Jason Manser. Shown here winning American Miniature Schnauzer Club Sweepstakes in Louisville, KY in 2006. Also won Reserve BIS at Bath (England), in an entry of 11,000. *Photo: Booth.*

Am. Ch. Repitition's Cornerstone: Breeder/Owner Kurt Garmaker. This son of Ch. Rampage's Representative was himself the sire of 76 Champions.

Sathgate Breakaway (27). Descendents from the Blue Spruce son Ch. Irrenhaus Blueprint (19) included Ch. Rampage's Kat Burglar (6), Ch. Rampage's Waco Kid (24), Ch. Irrenhaus Standout (21), Ch. Irrenhaus Sensation (19), and Ch. Irrenhaus Survivor (16). The impressive line of top-producing descendents continued through Carol Parker's own Skyline dogs, as well as in other kennels, including Abiqua, Adamis, Blythewood, Elete, Irrenhaus, Dimension, Dow, Kharasahl, Rampage, Repitition, and Regency.

## BANDSMAN

Carole Luke Weinberger's Bandsman dogs began when her first bitch, Jadee Wildflower, produced Ch. Bandsman's Sky Rocket in Flite (6) in 1975. He was then sold to Jerry Oldham of Jerry O's. Carole then purchased the bitch Ch. Repitition's Renaissance (8), who produced Ch. Bandsman's Bouquet (4). Bouquet, bred to Ch. Irrenhaus

Sensation in 1984 produced Ch. Bandsman's Talisman (7) and his three sisters, Ch. Bandsman's Cookie Bouquet (6), Ch. Bandsman's Free Spirit (11), and Ch. Bandsman's PostScript (5). Carole's association with Jerry Oldham in 1986, led to the black and silver Ch. Bandsman's Newsprint (38), who sired producers Ch. Bandsman Special Assignment (7), Ch. Pip'N Easy to Please (5), and Ch. Beucinder's Blackheath Brio (black/silver) (6). Bandsman dogs contributed to the success of Sumerwynd, Bojangles, Wards Creek, Pip 'N and others.

## RUEDESHEIM

Anne Lockney's Ruedesheim kennel showed the success that came from starting with the Delegate and Diplomat lines, and then adding the Ruffian lines. Started in the mid 1970s, Anne's Ruedesheim dogs have given many others a good start in Miniature Schnauzers, including Dynasty, Gangway, Shegar, Royalcourt, Tejas, and Premier. Special Ruedesheim producers include Ch. Ruedesheim's Entrepreneur (16), Ch. Ruedesheim's Momentumm (11), Ch. Ruedesheim Bonus (27) born in 1985, Ch. Ruedesheim's Fortune Seeker II (28) whelped in 1993, Ch. Ruedesheim's Advantage V Belgar (12), Ch. Ruedesheim's Billionaire (40), and Ch. Ruedesheim's Gigolo (11) who won four Bests in Show in 2003. The Best in Show bitch, Ch. Ruedesheim's I'm Precocious, was the first bitch to become Top Miniature Schnauzer. Two quality bitches, Ch. Ruedesheim's I'm Scrumptious and Ruedesheim's Heart's Delight, each produced 11 Champion offspring.

**Am. Ch. Ruedesheim's Billionaire: Breeder/Owner Anne Lockney. Billionaire sired 40 Champions, and became the Number Two Miniature Schnauzer in 1976.**

**Am. Ch. Ruedesheim's Bonus: Breeder/Owner Anne Lockney. This sire of 27 Champions, was the Number One sire in 1991.**

**Am. Ch. Rampage's Waco Kid (black & silver): Breeder Janice Ramel, Co-owners Janice Ramel and Carol and Kurt Garmaker. He was the sire of 24 Champions.**

**Am. Ch. Rampage's Representative: Breeder Janice Ramel, Co-owners Janice Ramel, Carol and Kurt Garmaker. Representative was the Number One Miniature Schnauzer for both 1990 & 1991. He won 17 Specialties, four All-Breed Bests in Show, 149 Group placements, including 49 Group Firsts, 54 Group Seconds, and sired 88 Champions.** *Photo: John Ashby.*

## RAMPAGE

Janice Ramel, Rampage, together with Kurt and Carol Garmaker of Repitition, worked to develop a most successful show and breeding programme. Janice Ramel's Ch. Rampage's Waco Kid, a black and silver whelped in 1982, did much to bring notice to that colour in the show ring through his 24 Champion offspring. Waco's top-producing son, Ch Jerry-O's Rain Check (black and silver) (17), sired Ch. Bandsman's Newsprint (black and silver)(38). Waco's grandson, Ch. Rampage's Express Mail

(38), bred to a Waco Kid daughter, resulted in one of the breed's all-time top sires, Ch. Rampage's Representative (88). Rep, whelped in 1988, was bred by Janice Ramel, and co-owned by Janice and Carol and Kurt Garmaker.

Through Rep came Ch. Repitition's Cornerstone (76), bred and owned by Kurt Garmaker. Additional Rep sons include Ch. Ruedesheim's Innocent Blush (11), Ch. Ruedesheim's Fortune Seeker II (28), Ch. Wy-O's Reputation (11), Ch. Repitition's Quixotic

One (black and silver) (17), and Ch. Regency's Absolut (11). Rep influence was felt through Awesome, Bojangles, Bravo, Chattelaine, Destineez, Dynasty, Far Hills, Gangway, Hardinhaus, Lewis, Liebestraum, Markworth, Nicknack, Regency, Royalcourt, Ruedesheim, T-Lan's, Wards Creek, Wy-O's and others.

## REGENCY

Beverly Verna, Regency, was fortunate to have Carol Parker as her mentor. Beverly's Ch. Marcheim Poppin' Fresh daughter, Jana PD, was bred to

Am. Ch. Regency's Right On Target: Breeder/Owner Beverly Verna. This Best in Show winner sired 78 Champions. In the show ring, he garnered 30 Group placements including 11 Firsts. He also earned 7 Specialty wins and 60 Best of Breed awards. *Photo: Carl Lindemeyer.*

Am. Ch. Regency's Twist of Fate: Co-Breeders/Co-Owners Beverly Verna and Gwen Mulheron. Twist of Fate won 11 Bests in Show, and sired 74 Champions.

Ch. Skyline's Blue Spruce in 1977 and produced Ch. Regency's Right On (34). Right On, bred to his full sister, Ch. Regency's Rosy Glow, produced Ch. Regency's Right On Target (78) in 1980. This very special dog made a critical impact on the development of Miniature Schnauzers throughout the world. Target sons include his black sons, Ch. Jubilee's Joker's Wild (9) and Ch. Regency's Shot in the Dark (5), as well as Ch. Sathgate Breakaway (27) whelped in 1982, Ch. Jadee's Royal Supershot (16), and many more

Champion children and grandchildren.

Beverly was the AKC's Terrier Group Breeder of the Year in 2006. Top-producing Regency dogs over the years include: Ch. Regency's Double Agent (10) whelped in 1989, Ch. Regency's Born to Boogie (10), and Ch. Regency's Absolut (11) in 1991. In 1999 came another very special dog, Ch. Regency's Twist of Fate (74). Twister was co-owned with Gwen Mulheron of Daree, home of Ch Jerry-O's Sharpshooter O'Daree (24).

John Constantine's Adamis'

best producer was Ch. Adamis Frontrunner (39), a son of Ch. Regency's Born to Boogie.

*CARMEL*

Carma Ewer, Carmel, made a good start with her Ch. Carmel Salute to Arepo (8), but it was her Twist of Fate son, born in 2003, Ch Hi-Line's Carmel with a Twist (19), who became the producer for her.

With a solid base such as these breeders have given us, Miniature Schnauzers in the US continue to flourish.

# A MINIATURE SCHNAUZER FOR YOUR LIFESTYLE

## Chapter 3

So, you are thinking of purchasing a Miniature Schnauzer? It's a big decision to make and should not be taken lightly. There are a lot of things to consider and it is important to weigh up both the pros and the cons.

Ask yourself the following questions:

- Is this breed right for you?
- Will a Miniature Schnauzer fit in with your family and your lifestyle?
- Will your work commitments allow you to give a Miniature Schnauzer the life he deserves?
- Do you have the finance to care for a dog – particularly one that needs frequent visits to the grooming parlour?
- Are you prepared to exercise your Miniature Schnauzer,

come rain or shine?
- Do you have time to dedicate to a puppy's training and socialisation?

Be sure to discuss the prospect of owning a Miniature Schnauzer with all the family. It has to be something that everyone wants to be involved with and – to a varying extent – take a share of the responsibility. There may be one person who is to be the prime carer, but what will happen if that person goes away on holiday, for example, or if their circumstances change? You need to think about the next 14 years, as this is the average lifespan of a Miniature Schnauzer.

### THE RIGHT BREED

The Miniature Schnauzer is an outstanding companion dog, but there are a few breed-specific

considerations to think about.

One of the Miniature Schnauzer's greatest attributes is the fact that his coat does not moult – which means that your house – and your clothes – will be free of dog hair. This is great news if you – or a member of your family – is allergic to dog hair, but it does not mean that the Mini is a low-maintenance breed – far from it. You will find that the profuse amount of leg hair will act as Velcro to any twigs and leaves, plus the legs and beard will need washing and brushing regularly in order to keep them in a mat-free condition. You will also need to budget for regular professional grooming, which, depending on where you live, can be rather costly.

The Miniature Schnauzer has few faults, but the breed is notoriously noisy. A Mini will let you know if there is anybody at the door, a cat or bird in the backyard or a dog barking three houses away. Before you purchase your puppy, please ensure that your neighbours are aware of your decision, because it could affect them, too. Fortunately, a Miniature Schnauzer will only bark if there is a reason; he will not bark if there is no stimulant. However, due to the fact that most houses have fairly close neighbours, the ambient noises of the neighbourhood will probably be enough to set him off.

## YOUR LIFESTYLE

As a breed, the Miniature Schnauzer is possibly one of the most versatile. He will pretty much adapt to any lifestyle and will, effortlessly, fit into your regime. Do not be fooled by his small size or the title 'Miniature' – if you have an active lifestyle, a Mini can quite happily cope with being on the go all day. However, he is equally at home sitting on his owner's knee in front of the fire.

A Miniature Schnauzer will be the perfect companion dog, regardless of your family make-up. But if you have small children, you will need to supervise interactions, as play can get out of hand very easily. This is an important consideration, and if you think it could be problematic, maybe you should wait until your children are a little older before bringing a dog into the family.

A Miniature Schnauzer will enhance your lifestyle, but you should be prepared for the fact that he will also inhibit the things you do. You cannot take off for a weekend away on the spur of the moment – unless you are going to friends who like dogs or you able to book dog-friendly accommodation. You may have a friend or a relative who could dog-sit for you, but this could be asking for trouble unless the person is experienced with dogs and could cope if an emergency arose.

The same problem arises if you want to go away on holiday – particularly if you plan to go abroad. There are many reputable boarding kennels, but you would need to inspect them and to book a place for your dog well in advance.

The ideal scenario is if you have the lifestyle where your Miniature Schnauzer can come on holiday with you. He will thoroughly enjoy the change of scene, and you will have fun taking him on new rambles or for games on the beach.

## WORK COMMITMENTS

Think about how much time you have for dog ownership – this is particularly important if you go out to work. If you are away from home all day, then leaving a puppy for long hours on his own is not advisable for a Miniature Schnauzer, or for any breed.

**The Miniature Schnauzer is always on the alert – ready to inform you of anything that is going on.**

Ideally, a puppy should have someone at home for most of the day, and an adult should not be left for longer than four hours at a time. If your work makes this impossible, you should seriously consider whether this is the right time for you to take on a dog. Very few, if any, good breeders would be willing to sell one of their puppies to a potential owner who is out for the whole day, however nice the family may be.

You could enlist the services of a dog walker or ask a neighbour to check on your Miniature Schnauzer during the day. This might be OK for an adult who has settled into a routine, but it is no good for a puppy. Puppies need around-the-clock attention in order to provide the correct training and socialisation, as well as building a bond with their human family.

Of course, there will be times when your Mini will have to be left alone; it would be impractical to think otherwise. However, these outings can coincide with times when your puppy is sleeping, and they can be kept to a minimum, particularly when the puppy is young. Make no mistake, taking on a puppy is a big commitment.

When your Miniature Schnauzer is older, you could consider an option such as doggy day care where your dog can be looked after in someone else's home. However, you would need to have complete confidence in the person running the service, and you would need to be satisfied that your dog was getting

**Will work commitments allow you to spend enough time with your Miniature Schnauzer?** Photo © istockphoto.com/Daniel Rodriguez.

sufficient exercise and mental stimulation during the day. If you are going to need day care on a regular basis, it will prove to be quite costly.

### FINANCE

It may seem cold-blooded to work out what your dog is going to cost you during the course of his lifetime, but it would be imprudent to go ahead with acquiring a Miniature Schnauzer if you could not afford to keep him.

Obviously, you will need the purchase price, and you will need to buy equipment, such as a dog

crate and grooming equipment (see Chapter Four), but it is the on-going expenses that you will need to budget for. These will include:

- **Food:** This will not be a huge expense for a breed the size of a Miniature Schnauzer, but you need to be able to provide a good-quality balanced diet to suit your dog's individual needs throughout his life.
- **Health care:** You can take out insurance to cover unexpected veterinary bills, but you need to make sure you can afford the monthly or annual premium.

It is a bonus if you can take your Mini on holiday – but if that is not possible you will have to make suitable arrangements.

You will also need to pay for routine preventive health care, which will include vaccinations as well as flea and worming treatment.

- **Grooming:** Unless you plan to get involved in showing, which involves the laborious process of handstripping the coat, your Miniature Schnauzer will need clipping every six weeks.

  *For more information, see Chapter Five: The Best of Care.*

- **Work cover:** if you work more than four hours a day – and there is no one else at home – you will need to budget for professional help.

- **Holidays:** If you plan to go away without your dog, you will need to employ the services of a dog sitter or pay for boarding kennels.

## WHAT DO YOU WANT FROM YOUR MINIATURE SCHNAUZER?

When considering a Miniature Schnauzer, you need to decide what you, and your family, require from a dog. Would you like a pet who can shadow you everywhere you go? Would you like a potential show dog, or maybe you would like to get involved in one of the dog sports, such as agility or obedience? Do you want to go rough-shooting with your dog?

Traditionally, Miniature Schnauzers were bred as farm dogs and carried out jobs such as 'ratting'. However, nowadays the majority of Schnauzers are bred purely for the pet market. So if you wanted a farm dog to control vermin, then a Miniature Schnauzer would probably not be

at the top of your list of suitable breeds.

### PET DOG

As a pet, there is no breed more suited to the role. The Miniature Schnauzer is a fun breed and loves to please. He is naturally obedient and always has a happy demeanour. He will love all the family, and is great with children and with other dogs.

### SHOW DOG

If you are looking for a show dog, then contact one of your local breed clubs and go along to the next show in your area. Have a good look at all the dogs presented in the ring. You will start to see differences in type – even a novice with no show experience will start to pick out a

**You will need expert help if you want to get involved in showing.**

**This is a breed that has really made its mark in agility.**

type that best pleases their eye. When you have decided on what you like, take a look in the catalogue to see if the breeder lives within a reasonable distance, and, hopefully, you can arrange a visit to find out more.

You will need a lot of help when you first start showing; the grooming involved is an art form in itself, and you will also need to train your dog for the ring. Therefore, if you can find a local breeder that is willing to mentor you, then you have a good start.

## SPORTS DOG
Although a Miniature Schnauzer probably would not be the first breed you would consider if you were hoping for an agility or obedience dog – they have proved to be very talented in both of these fields. There have been Minis all around the world who have won the top accolades in both agility and obedience.

If you are thinking of a field working dog, then a Miniature Schnauzer would probably not be your ideal choice. He has never been bred to retrieve, and although a Miniature Schnauzer will tolerate a game of 'fetch' for so long, he will soon tire of it. The coat furnishings would pose a

major problem if your dog needed to run through thicket, gorse or woodland, as they tend to tangle and matt.

## MALE OR FEMALE?
With Minis there really is very little difference between a male or a female. It is very rare – almost unheard of – for dominance issues to occur, and you will find that the males will be just as loving and sociable as the females.

The males are marginally bigger; they have outgoing, fun personalities and rarely show aggression towards other dogs. Obviously, a male has no 'season' to contend with, but some may, occasionally, mark their territory by cocking their leg. This is unlikely to happen in your home, but it may occur if you are visiting friends or family, particularly if they have a female dog in residence.

The females are more feminine in appearance; they are fun-loving and affectionate. You will have to cope with a female's seasonal cycle. This generally occurs twice a year, and a season lasts for around three weeks. During this time she will need to be kept away from males to avoid the risk of an unplanned pregnancy.

If you do not want to get involved in breeding, you may consider neutering your Miniature Schnauzer, which can have health benefits as well as being more convenient. The best plan is to discuss this with your vet.

## WHAT COLOUR?

There are four recognised Miniature Schnauzer colours in the UK and Europe. These are pepper and salt, black and silver, black, and the recently added white, although this is not recognised in the USA.

Pepper and salt is the most common; if you want one of the other colours – particularly white – you may have to put your name on a waiting list with a breeder that specialises in the colour you want.

## FINDING A BREEDER

I would like to say that it is easy to find a responsible breeder that produces sound, healthy, typical Miniature Schnauzers. But I have to admit that it's a minefield out there. For every good breeder, there are a handful of underhand puppy farmers, who have no interest in the breed, except to make a fast buck. Therefore, you need to be very careful and research the topic thoroughly.

The best way of finding a reputable breeder is to join your local Miniature Schnauzer club. You can find a list of these on the internet. In the UK, the main one is The Miniature Schnauzer Club, and in the USA, it is the American Miniature Schnauzer Club or AMSC. These clubs will have a list of breeders in your area, which you can use as a reference point, so that even if they have no puppies available, they may know of another breeder locally who does. You can also ask to be directed to an upcoming Miniature Schnauzer dog show. Try to get to one of these events as part of your research, as most breeders are more than willing to give advice and you can gain some invaluable information.

Try to avoid breeders that breed on a large scale with numerous different breeds.

Lastly, be very careful when buying from the internet. There are some fabulous breeder websites out there and the majority are what they say they

**Pepper and salt is the easiest colour to find.**

**You want to find a breeder who has a reputation for producing sound, healthy puppies that are typical of the breed.**

are. However, this is not always the case. Fancy wording and spruced-up photos can give an impression of credibility that is not based on hard evidence. It is all too easy to fall in love with a photo of a sweet-looking puppy, but you have no information about the breeder, the bloodlines that have been used, or how the puppies have been reared.

When you have tracked down a litter, you need to make an appointment to view the puppies. In most cases, a breeder will not want visitors until the puppies are five to six weeks old because of the risk of infection or upsetting the dam. It is also important to wait until the puppies are fully mobile and you can make a proper assessment of their looks and their personalities.

Always ask to see the mother with her puppies, and the area in which the puppies were reared. Never arrange to meet a breeder at the side of a road or away from their kennel, unless you have first-hand knowledge of how the puppy had been reared and in what conditions. Never take the breeder's word that the puppy has been well cared for; you need to see this for yourself.

In order to ensure that the puppy you are buying is a purebred, it is imperative that the puppy is Kennel Club (UK)/American Kennel Club (USA) registered. If it is not registered, there is no guarantee that you are getting a genuine, purebred puppy.

Miniature Schnauzers are now one of the most popular breeds, due to their wonderful nature and few health issues. However the negative side to this is that there are far too many breeders who are producing puppies purely for profit.

## ASSESSING A LITTER

All puppies are irresistible, so how do you decide which one to choose when you go to see a litter? The answer is quite simple: it depends on what you want your puppy to do. Do you want a pet, a dog to show, or maybe an agility competitor? You need a clear view in your mind from the beginning.

If you are buying a pet, then it may be that the breeder has already decided which puppies from the litter are to be kept back for the show ring or for agility trials. It may be that you have the choice of several of the remaining puppies, or that there is only one puppy left. Either way, you want to be sure that the puppy you take home with you is sound and healthy. This is where the difficulty lies. How can you assess the puppies for health, temperament and conformation?

Firstly, make sure you arrange to see the litter when the puppies are likely to be at their most active. If they spend most of the morning running around but then collapse in the afternoon, you need to see them in the morning. All puppies should be full of life and active if you catch them when they are awake. It may be best to visit on several occasions, because a puppy can sometimes be quiet due to teething, especially around eight weeks of age, which is when the milk teeth start to break through. Be prepared that if you get the timing wrong, you may arrive and one or two of the puppies may seem quiet – they have probably been manic just 20 minutes beforehand but are now flagging and want to sleep. This is very different to a puppy who has not had any early socialisation or stimulants and is cowering at the back of the pen. If you see a whole litter that is frightened and nervy, *beware!* Puppies should be happy and outgoing, craving fuss and attention from people – when not fighting their littermates, of course.

Ask the breeder if you can see the whelping room and nursery. It should be clean and smell fresh – and there should be plenty of toys for the puppies to play with. As well as being active, the puppies should show the following signs of good health:

- Bright eyes with no signs of discharge.
- Well covered but not pot-bellied, as this could indicate the presence of worms.
- No crustiness on the nose and no discharge from it.
- Healthy-looking coat with no bald patches or dandruff.
- Clean rear end – matting of the fur could indicate diarrhoea.

It is not always possible to see the sire of the litter, as the breeder may have used a dog from another kennel. However, you should be able to see his pedigree and some photos. Of course, you will want to see the mother and any other close relatives. As a breeder, I want prospective puppy purchasers to meet all my dogs, as this will help them to find out what sort of temperament they prefer. You cannot always tell at eight weeks how each puppy will mature but the breeder, who will have spent many hours watching the litter, will have a feel for their individual personalities. For example, you may get a puppy who is smaller than the others, but more than makes up for it in attitude, or there may be a larger puppy who is laid back and spends more time lazing around sleeping.

## ASK QUESTIONS

Finally, do not be afraid to ask questions. A breeder should be proud to show off their dogs, run through their pedigrees, and give

**How do you pick a puppy that is going to suit you and your family?**

# EYE EXAMS

As a rule, Miniature Schnauzers are a healthy breed. However, there are several hereditary eye problems that can occur. In order to try to eliminate these from the breed, an annual eye examination can be carried out; this is particularly important for breeding stock. In the UK, the examinations are run through the British Veterinary Association and the Kennel Club; in the US, the Canine Eye Registration Foundation provides a database of dogs who have been examined by the diplomates of the American College of Veterinary Ophthalmologists.

The hereditary diseases associated with the Miniature Schnauzer are:

**Congenital juvenile cataracts:** Cataracts will affect a dog in a similar way to how humans are affected, by clouding up the lens of the eye and blurring the vision. Due to a recessive gene (a gene that is hidden), cataracts can occur in young Miniature Schnauzers.

**Progressive retinal atrophy (PRA):** PRA is an inherited disease that occurs in most breeds including the Miniature Schnauzer. The retina deteriorates over a period of time (a year or so), which means that there is a gradual loss of sight, starting with night blindness and often resulting in full blindness.

**Retinal dysplasia (RD):** Retinal dysplasia is a genetic defect where the retina ranges from being folded, to (in extreme cases) being detached. The severity of the condition will determine the degree of blindness. Retinal dysplasia can be diagnosed in an eight-week-old puppy.

Always ensure that both of the parents of your prospective puppy hold a clear eye exam and the litter has also been screened for any hereditary eye deformities. The last thing any pet owner needs is to take on a dog who loses his sight at an early age. (See also page 144)

you details of their show records and other achievements, both past and present.

Make sure that you have determined the purchase price and whether a deposit is required. You also need to find out if there are any endorsements attached to the sale. For example, a breeder may impose breeding or export restrictions on the

puppies. Therefore, if you would like your bitch puppy to have a litter when she matures, you need to discuss this with the breeder when you purchase the puppy. Some breeders may stipulate that the puppy is never bred from. Likewise, if you plan on moving abroad in the near future, be sure to discuss this with the breeder.

## SHOW POTENTIAL

If you want to get involved in showing, you need to approach a breeder who is already breeding for good construction and an outgoing temperament. Go to a dog show and assess the dogs being shown. Decide which type you like and find out if there are any puppies available with those lines. It is highly unlikely that you

A Champion in the making: This is Ch. Zakmayo Rula Thumb aged eight weeks. Rula went on to become Top Miniature Schnauzer in 2010 and the Bitch CC Winner and Best Opposite Sex (BOS) at Crufts 2011. If you want to choose a dog to show, the breeder will help you to choose a puppy with show potential.

as an adult. Take lots of photos of the puppy stacked, and study each and every puppy against his littermates.

When stacked in a show stance, does the puppy give an appearance of balance? Miniature Schnauzer construction consists of a lot of measurements that balance throughout. For example, the dog should appear square (or nearly square), meaning that the length of the body should equal the height at the withers. The angulation of the shoulder should equal the angulation of the hindquarters. The depth of body should equal the length of leg. The puppy should possess a forechest, and the head should resemble a brick.

If the milk teeth are through, check that the top jaw is more forward than the lower jaw, so that when your puppy matures, he will end up with the correct scissor bite. If the pup is a male that you plan to show, check that there are two testicles.

It is hard to tell what the coat will be like at eight weeks. However, sometimes you can see some harsh hair (generally light in colour) already growing under the puppy coat. When the puppy is running around, take a look at how the puppy trots along. You need to see a clean action in front, where the front legs move perfectly straight without swinging in or out. With regards to rear action, look for a puppy who moves with a wide rear, as this will narrow with age.

Above all, take a copy of the

will buy a Miniature Schnauzer with show potential from a pet breeder, who has no knowledge of correct construction or the show ring. However, it is important to bear in mind that even if you buy a puppy which possesses the best pedigree in the country, there are no guarantees, and the most promising puppy may not make the grade as an adult.

In order to pick out the best puppy for the job, you need to take an experienced person along with you or trust the breeder you

are purchasing from. It takes years and years to learn what to look for in a potential show dog, and even with all this experience, a breeder can still get it wrong.

To produce a list of attributes of what to look for in a show dog is no easy task; you could write a whole book on the subject and still only touch the surface. However, here are some basic guidelines:

First and foremost, you need to look at the puppy as a whole at eight weeks. What you see at eight weeks is often what you see

Breed Standard along with you and grade each point of the dog according to the Standard. This will give you a good idea of whether the puppy is likely to make it as a show dog. You need to be super critical, because the faults you see at eight weeks will still be there as an adult.

Once you have chosen your puppy, be prepared that he may go through 'the uglies' as he matures. This is quite normal and can last right up to 18 months old with some lines, so be patient.

## TAKING ON AN OLDER DOG

Occasionally a breeder may be prepared to sell an older dog. It may be that a bitch has retired from breeding or a youngster is not quite right for the show ring but will make a great pet dog. Miniature Schnauzers are so adaptable, they will settle with anyone who offers them a warm home, a soft lap and a delicious meal. If you want to miss out on the puppy stage, this could be an ideal solution, as it is very rare for a Miniature Schnauzer to have problems settling into a new home.

**It may suit you to miss out on the puppy stage and take on an older dog.**

## RESCUED DOGS

Due to the increasing popularity of the breed, there are now more and more Miniature Schnauzers that end up in rescue, needing a second chance to find a loving home. Often this is due to bereavement or family circumstances changing (such as marriage break-up), rather than an inability to cope with the dog. If you would like to rehome a Miniature Schnauzer, it is best to contact the breed clubs, such as The Miniature Schnauzer Club (UK) or the American Miniature Schnauzer Club (USA) for details of a local rescue group.

In some cases, you may be able to take a rescued dog on a month's trial to see if he will fit in with your family and your lifestyle.

# THE NEW ARRIVAL

## Chapter 4

Once you have decided that the Miniature Schnauzer is the breed for you, it will come as a pleasant surprise that you will find a lot more in this little package than just good looks.

The Miniature Schnauzer is classed as a terrier in the USA, but in the UK the breed is listed in the all-purpose Utility Group. This can lead to some confusion but, to my mind, the Miniature Schnauzer should not be compared to a terrier breed, as the temperament is completely different.

A Miniature Schnauzer is quite capable of catching mice and can stand his corner if needs be, but generally this is a very happy breed and likes to join in with everything you do. He is a true family dog, and is also sociable with other dogs. He is content to live in a one-dog family or in a mini pack.

The Miniature Schnauzer is tough and quite robust in body, and enjoys as much or as little exercise as you are able to give him. A Miniature Schnauzer may look bristling and alert, but at home he is a real softie and loves his cuddles.

This extremely intelligent breed is also very biddable. He is quick to learn and will pick up tricks and party pieces in no time. The Miniature Schnauzer also has a stubborn streak and will become easily bored with monotonous repetition. It is important to bear this in mind when you are planning a training session.

I have found my Miniature Schnauzers to be very faithful and loving. They are also very sensitive when reprimanded and will sulk for a long time or give the impression of having hurt feelings. They thrive on lots of affection from all members of the family, but will have their preferences as to whom they like best.

## CHOOSING A PUPPY

When you first look at a litter of eight-week-old puppies, they all seem identical. which can be a little daunting.

If you are looking for a companion rather than a potential show dog, the best plan is to ask the breeder to help you choose the pup that is most likely to suit your lifestyle. Over the weeks of rearing the litter, the breeder will have seen the puppies develop and will have got to know their individual personalities. Even at this early stage, there may be significant differences in character, so it is important to match a puppy with a family where he is

**Look at your home from a puppy's perspective and try to eliminate potential hazards.**

going to thrive. For example, a quiet or more reserved puppy would be much happier with an older person or with a one-to-one relationship, whereas a very playful puppy will enjoy a family life or will be suited to a more active person.

## PREPARATION FOR THE NEW PUPPY

When you are waiting for your new puppy, you can fill in time by preparing your home and garden for the new arrival.

*IN THE HOME*
An inquisitive Miniature

Schnauzer puppy will be keen to explore every nook and cranny of his new home, so you must work hard at ensuring the environment is as safe as possible.

In truth, it is impossible to make a home 100 per cent safe, so the best plan is to allocate a safe area where your puppy can be confined at times when you cannot supervise him. This may take the form of a crate, or you can set up a play-pen (see pages 48 and 49). It is also a good idea to put up some baby-gates, such as at the bottom of stairs or at the kitchen door, so you can restrict your puppy when needed. As you

puppy gets older – and more trustworthy – you can allow him more freedom.

Before you collect your puppy, you should decide where your new puppy is going to sleep. He will need lots of rest over the next few months while he is growing, so it is very important that he has a place where he feels safe and secure.

The best option is to buy an indoor crate, which can be located in a convenient corner – most people find the kitchen or utility room works best. It is important that the place you choose is free from draughts; it should be warm in the winter and not too hot in the summer months.

A young puppy will chew, and although you may provide him with toys and dog chews, he will always find things that are more fun. Electric cables are a potential hazard, so these must be secured out of reach, or the puppy should not be allowed in rooms where there are trailing cables from electrical equipment, such as computers and printers. Chewing tends to be at its worst when a puppy is teething – at around four months of age. Likely items are shoes, mats, curtains, and sometimes hard, wooden objects, such as table-legs. House plants are another temptation; a puppy can cause a great deal of mess if he pulls down a plant, and there is an added danger, as the plant may well be poisonous to dogs.

In my experience, some puppies chew everything they can get hold of, while others cause

**A Mini puppy has no sense of danger so you will need to fence off potential hazards.**

few problems. The best advice is to confine your puppy to a crate or a playpen when you cannot supervise him properly.

Puppies also love to tug on things, so be vigilant when your puppy is in the kitchen. Hanging tea towels by a hot stove are very tempting to pull down and play with. In fact, the kitchen is full of potential hazards, and I would suggest that a puppy has no place in the kitchen, unless he is in a crate or in a sectioned-off area. It may work best if you put up a gate in the doorway of the kitchen; the puppy will still see you but he will not get under your feet.

In many ways, a puppy should be treated like a small child – anything that might be harmful to a small child could be as harmful to your pup.

*IN THE GARDEN*
Before your puppy arrives home, check the fencing in your garden to make sure it is secure. Although the Miniature Schnauzer is very agile, he is not a natural escapologist. He would rather strut around the boundaries than spend time trying to escape. However, you can never take risks with a puppy.

An inquisitive puppy will find the smallest gap to get through

and once he has escaped he will always have to be watched, as he will do it again.

A puppy will explore his environment with his mouth, which means he will pick up and chew anything he comes across – even small stones and pieces of plastic. If you are a keen gardener, you will find that nothing is safe – and there are also a number of shrubs and plants that are toxic to dogs.

You will also need to check how you store your rubbish. Rubbish bags are irresistible to the ever-hungry Miniature Schnauzer, but eating leftover food and other rubbish could be disastrous.

# PLANTS TO AVOID

Low, spiky plants that can cause eye injuries.

**Poisonous plants**
- Laburnum (also the seed pods)
- Lupins (also the seed pods)
- Poinsettia leaves
- Rhododendron leaves
- Ivy
- Holly berries
- Jasmine leaves
- Foxgloves – stems and leaves
- Clematis – stems and leaves.

*For a comprehensive list of toxic plants, check on the internet.*

An additional hazard is a garden pond, which appears fascinating to a young puppy, but is potentially lethal.

If you have a reasonably large garden, it would be best to have an area that you can section off as a puppy play area. Ideally, this would be partially shaded, so your pup can enjoy the fresh air without getting too hot. It is also important to provide a bowl of drinking water in the play area, and make sure you replace it on a daily basis.

You can also use part of the play area for toileting – if your puppy is taken to the same spot every time he is taken out, he will soon learn what is required.

## BUYING EQUIPMENT

There are a few essential items of equipment you will need to buy for your new puppy:

### INDOOR CRATE

I recommend all my new owners to buy an indoor crate for the puppy; it is an investment. but it has many uses and will give you the great gift of peace of mind.

A crate can be used:
- At times when you cannot supervise your puppy
- To keep him safe overnight
- As a safe means of transport in the car
- When visiting friends in non-doggy homes
- In hotels and rented holiday accommodation

Indoor crates come in a range of different sizes, but it is best to buy one that will be the correct

**An indoor crate provides a place of safety for your puppy.**

size for your Miniature Schnauzer when he is a mature adult. I suggest buying a metal crate, preferably with two doors, measuring 20 inches wide, 24 inches long and 21 inches deep (51 cm x 61 cm x 53 cm).

## PLAYPEN

A playpen is an added extra that is so useful when your puppy is in the early stages of growing up. It can be used in the home and can also be used outside in the summer months.

The playpen comes in specially made wire-mesh panels and can be fitted to the required size. The panels can be used to section off parts of the house – or parts of the garden you do not want your puppy to go.

Mischievous puppies need constant supervision and it is impossible to watch them all the time. In a playpen, a puppy is in a safe place where he cannot harm himself – and is not under your feet – but he can watch everything that is going on around him and not feel left out.

## BEDDING

The crate will need to be lined with cosy bedding. The best type to buy is synthetic fleece, which is sold in most pet shops and can be cut to any size. The fabric is made so that wet patches soak through to the base, which means that the bed is always dry. The bedding is machine-washable and lasts a long time. You will need more than one piece of bedding, as it will need changing most days. You can add a warm jumper of your

There is a range of beds to choose from – but you may be advised to wait until your puppy has stopped chewing before making a major investment.

own or a warm water bottle at night to help as a comforter.

## DOG BED

In addition to an indoor crate, your Miniature Schnauzer will appreciate a dog bed as he gets older. This can be located in a room, such as the sitting room, where the family gathers, giving your Miniature Schnauzer his own place to settle within the family circle.

The best type to buy is a hard, plastic bed that can be lined with synthetic fleece bedding. This type of bed is virtually indestructible – even for the most determined of chewers! It is also easy to keep clean.

There are lots of attractive soft and cosy beds on the market, but these are unlikely to last long with a Miniature Schnauzer. He will be tempted to give his bed a good shake, and as well as testing your patience, he may well choke on

the inner stuffing or the polyester beads, which will spread for miles!

## BOWLS

Feeding bowls and water bowls come in all shapes and sizes, and in a range of colours and materials. The best types to buy are those made of stainless steel with a wide bottom and rubber grip. These are spill-proof and can be washed easily in hot, soapy water.

However, in the first few weeks it may be worth buying a deep, plastic bowl for your puppy. Some pups can be alarmed by the clatter of stainless steel, particularly if their ID tag bangs against the side. I have known some puppies who have been reluctant to feed because of this.

For an adult Miniature Schnauzer, I would recommend a heavy stoneware bowl for water. For puppies, you will need a shallow, spill-proof bowl, and the water will need to be refreshed on a regular basis.

For garden use, you can buy a bowl that attaches to the fence; again, make sure the water is kept fresh.

### COLLARS AND LEADS

The first collar for a puppy needs to be lightweight and narrow. He will only use this for a short time to get used to wearing a collar. Make sure both the collar and the lead (which should be made of lightweight nylon) have secure fastening.

You may also wish to invest in an extending lead, which will give your puppy – and adult – more freedom while still remaining under your control.

It is a matter of personal preference what you would like your Miniature Schnauzer to wear when he is older. Some owners opt for a standard leather collar for everyday use, and a half-chain collar when out walking. You will want a stronger lead than the lightweight puppy lead, but the choice is up to you, as long as it has a secure trigger fastening.

### GROOMING GEAR

For most owners, having a well-groomed dog is a matter of personal pride. This is particularly the case with the high-maintenance coat of a Miniature Schnauzer. You will need to start off with some basic equipment and add to it as the coat grows. Obviously, the equipment you need will depend on whether you are using the services of a grooming parlour.

For a puppy, you will need the following equipment:
- A small, soft slicker brush
- A small, fine comb
- A large metal comb
- Nail clippers
- Toothbrush and toothpaste.

*For more information on grooming, see Chapter Five: The Best of Care.*

### TOYS

There is a huge variety of toys you can buy – but the overriding consideration is that they are safe. A puppy can chew through soft fabric and plastic with ease, and if pieces of the toy are swallowed, the results can be disastrous. The best type to buy are those made of hard rubber, such as Kongs (which can also be stuffed with food), and cotton tug toys. Balls with bells inside

**You will need to provide some robust toys – or your puppy will find his own amusement!**

need to be quite big, as they could be a choking hazard if they are too small or made of sponge.

However, you will find that your pup soon gets bored with his toys, so rather than spending a fortune on items from the pet shop, there are a few safe homemade toys you can provide that will cost you nothing:

- Sturdy, plastic flowerpots that are big enough so that a puppy will not get his head stuck.
- A sock tied in the middle, or an old rope tied in knots, for a great tug-of-war game.
- Place a few treats in a plastic bottle and leave the top off. A puppy will have great fun trying to extract the treats.
- There are lots of safe, cuddly toys you can get from charity shops. A toy that is safe for a baby will be safe for a puppy; anything with glass eyes or with synthetic hair is not recommended. The other cuddly toys to avoid, unless supervised, are toys stuffed with polyester beads.

Keep a regular check on all the toys to see they are safe and intact.

## CHEWS

Your puppy will also appreciate some dog chews, particularly when he is teething. Most of the hide chews are safe, but they need to be taken away when they have become damp. Make sure you buy the long, straight chews, as they do not break up into small pieces.

## ID

Identity tags come in all shapes and sizes, though some are more durable than others. It is best to get a strong metal tag that has been engraved with your telephone number and also stating that the puppy has been microchipped. Most owners do not include their dog's name, but this is a matter of choice.

Microchipping is a permanent form of ID. The chip is the size of a large grain of rice and is implanted under the skin. It contains your personal contact details and can be 'read' by a scanner. Implanting the chip is a simple procedure, usually performed by a vet.

## FINDING A VET

Before taking your puppy home, it is a good idea to ask friends or local dog owners which veterinary practice they would recommend. Most dog owners prefer their nearest vet for convenience, but it is a good idea to visit the practice to make sure it suits your needs.

Check out the following:
- Does the practice run an appointment system?
- What are the arrangements for emergency out-of-hours cover?
- What facilities are available on the premises?
- Do any of the vets have experience with Miniature Schnauzers?

**Ideally, your Miniature Schnauzer should wear an ID tag, and also have a tag stating that he has been microchipped.**

- What is the policy on complementary therapies?
- Is the receptionist friendly and helpful?

It is important that you are happy with the way the practice is run, as you never know when you are going to need help and support.

The first time you visit the practice, your puppy will be given a check-up and he will probably be given his first vaccination. This can be done as early as eight weeks old; the second jab will be done two weeks later. Your new veterinary practice will also give you advice if you have any worries in the early days with your new puppy and also recommend where to go for your first socialisation classes.

It is always beneficial to have a relaxed and happy relationship with your vet. In times of need, the vet and his staff are there to help, and their expertise is very much appreciated.

## COLLECTING YOUR PUPPY

Today is the day you have been waiting for! Although you are very excited, you may also feel just a little nervous, wondering how you will cope will such a tiny 'baby'.

If this is your first Miniature Schnauzer, you will be amazed how quickly your puppy will make himself feel at home. All he needs is some reassurance and he will simply get on with life in his new home. If you have not had a puppy for a while, do not be alarmed, as the breeder will always help with any problems that are concerning you. You can be sure that your little bundle will soon be showing you what to do, when to do it, and where! His life will be governed by times to eat, sleep, walk, play and be cuddled.

Choose a time to collect your new puppy so that he has time to settle in his new home before bedtime. Late morning is a good time, as you can then give him a small feed when you get home.

Take a friend with you to collect your puppy, as he will be happy to be cuddled and sleep most of the way home. He may find the car strange and be a little sick, so take some paper towels with you. However, most Miniature Schnauzers travel well.

If you have to do the journey alone, prepare a deep cardboard box with a cosy blanket and a warm water bottle wrapped in a towel or blanket, and your puppy will be fine. When your puppy is settled, you can introduce him to travelling in a crate in the car, which is the safest means of transport.

## ARRIVING HOME

When you first arrive home, your puppy will be ready for a drink of water. He will also need to relieve himself after the journey. Take him to the area you have allocated, and when he performs, give him plenty of praise.

Arriving in a new home is a daunting experience for the most

**After all the hard work of rearing a litter, it is time for the breeder to say goodbye to the puppies.**

confident of puppies. Give your pup a chance to explore his new environment, giving reassurance so that he learns to recognise your voice and starts to feel relaxed. Miniature Schnauzer puppies are very outgoing and need no encouragement to investigate their surroundings.

## INTRODUCING THE CRATE

The best way to introduce a puppy to a crate is to locate it where the puppy plays and leave all his favourite things inside so he can go in and out as he wants. Make sure there is a cosy bed for him in the crate and he will use it for his naps as well as going in his dog bed.

Your puppy will find that a warm water bottle, wrapped in a towel, is a great comforter for a few days until he settles into his new surroundings.

Another way to encourage the puppy to be confined for short periods of time is to feed him in the crate and let him out after a few minutes. He will soon go in and out without fear and will use the crate as his safe place. Do not shut him in for long periods of time, as the crate should be viewed as an extra-safe zone – not a place where your puppy objects to being confined.

The breeder will have trained the puppies to toilet on paper, and you can use some paper

**Take time introducing your puppy to his crate so he learns to accept it as his own special den.**

bedding for this purpose if you want.

If you are using a playpen, you will find it very useful in the first few days, as it will give the pup a chance to get used to his new surroundings from the safety and security of his own base.

## MEETING THE FAMILY

When you first take your puppy home, he will be excited to meet his new family. Try not to excite him too much. If the atmosphere is calm, he will take everything in and start to feel at home much sooner.

There should be one person in the family who is in charge of feeding and toilet training, and generally supervising the new arrival. This allows for consistency in the first few weeks, and once the puppy is settled, everyone can join in and help.

The most important thing is to

establish a good routine so the puppy knows what to expect – and what is expected of him. In this way a puppy learns his place in the family, and anxieties are kept to a minimum.

## INTRODUCING CHILDREN

If the puppy is going to a family with children, try to keep them in the background to start with. Once the puppy has started to settle into his new surroundings, he will become more inquisitive and will build up the confidence to approach the children himself. A Miniature Schnauzer thrives on affection and once he realises he will have lots of cuddles, the bonding will have already started.

Young children should always be supervised when interacting with a puppy, and they also need to be taught how to behave with a dog from an early age:

• Children must be calm and not excite the puppy too much or he might start playing roughly and scratch with his nails or nip with his sharp, baby teeth.
• Loud shouting or screaming should also be discouraged, as this could make the puppy apprehensive or fearful.
• Children should always sit on the floor to play with the pup rather than attempting to pick him up – puppies are very wriggly and it is all too easy for an accident to happen.

- A puppy will explore by using his mouth to feel, touch and taste, so make sure children are equipped with puppy toys, so he does not nip fingers by mistake.
- A puppy gets tired very quickly, so children must not disturb the puppy when he makes for his crate or dog bed.

An older child can pick up a puppy if necessary, but this must be done in the correct way. All the body weight should be taken from under the tummy in one hand, with the other hand on the top to stop the puppy jumping out of your arms. However, it is best to keep lifting to a minimum, and go down to floor level to play with the puppy.

**Supervise interactions with small children, as accidents happen all too easily.**

### THE RESIDENT DOG
If you already have a dog, you will need to supervise early interactions with a new puppy to ensure relations get off on the right footing. If possible, introduce them in the garden, which will be viewed as neutral territory.

I suggest you hold the puppy in your arms to begin with and let the older dog sniff him. He will quickly realise that the 'interloper' is only a baby and poses no threat. The next step is to put the puppy in a confined area – ideally in the garden – so the adult dog cannot get to the pup but can socialise through the divider. Allow the adult dog complete freedom to approach the puppy and see what happens. In most cases, the adult will decide to ignore the puppy or will want to play. Puppies are very tough, but an adult can be rough, so play sessions must always be supervised until your puppy is a little bigger and stronger.

Puppies are taught by their mother to respect their elders, and you will discover that your puppy is equipped with the correct body language to communicate with an adult dog. If your adult dog appears to be friendly and is not worried by the puppy, you can let them out together. You will see that, within seconds, the puppy will roll over on his back in a gesture of surrender. He is showing that he accepts the older dog as boss. When the adult dog has accepted the puppy, they will run together and all should be well. While this first playtime is in progress, you must stop any rough play from the dog that would hurt the puppy. But try not to interfere too much, as it is important that they work out their own relationship.

### THE FAMILY CAT
If you have a cat – or cats – in your household, you will need to make plans before your puppy arrives. Firstly, earmark which areas of the house your cats like to use as their resting places. You must make these places safe for them, restricting the puppy's access so the cats are still free to come and go as they please.

For the first introduction, keep your puppy in his crate so he can see the cats – and they can see him – but no one feels

It is best to allow a puppy and an adult dog to establish their own relationship.

A Miniature Schnauzer can learn to live in harmony with the family cat – but it may take some time.

threatened. Section off areas so the puppy can watch the cats but cannot chase them. Once the cats know the puppy cannot get to them, they will move quite freely and cause little disturbance.

Once the novelty has worn off, the puppy will lose his fascination, and the cats will tend to divert and go to other safe areas when he is around. In time, they will learn to exist in mutual harmony – in some cases, they may even become friends.

## HOUSE RULES
When the family – and other animals – have been introduced,

it is time to all agree on the house rules. Where the puppy is, and is not, permitted to go must be agreed by all – and everyone must stick to the rules. If you break one of the rules and let him get on the sofa, for example, you will find he will do it again, thinking that he is not doing anything wrong. A puppy relies on your leadership to show him how to behave and how to fit in with your lifestyle.

## THE FIRST MEAL
It is important to stick to the diet your puppy has been getting from the breeder – for the first few weeks at least – in order to avoid

stomach upsets. A puppy has so much to get used to when he arrives in his new home, it is important to keep changes to a minimum. Read the diet sheet provided by the breeder and try to follow the instructions with regard to mealtimes and quantities as closely as possible.

Most tummy upsets in young puppies are caused by over feeding. This is so easy to do because puppies always seem to be hungry, but the truth is that they will always eat as much as you are prepared to give them.

If your Miniature Schnauzer has an upset tummy but appears well and is eating his meals, it is most likely you are over feeding. In this situation, it is a good idea to miss the next mealtime, as this will give the puppy's tummy time to settle. His next meal should be a small one.

If your puppy continues to have diarrhoea, or his stomach upset lasts more than one day, you must go to your vet for expert advice. It could be that it is a viral problem or something that will need medical treatment. A small puppy can become very ill very quickly, so if you are concerned, do not delay in seeking help.

If your puppy seems reluctant to eat, but seems well in himself, you can try adding a spoonful of canned meat or a little gravy on his food. This will get him started again and encourage his appetite. But once he has eaten this, go back to his usual diet or you will encourage him to become a picky feeder.

## THE FIRST NIGHT

If you have done all the preliminary preparations, your new Miniature Schnauzer puppy should hopefully not be too unsettled when it comes to bedtime. However, his first night in a new environment is a big step. He has had the rest of the litter to cuddle up to and now finds himself all alone.

This is where you need to give him the reassurance he needs so you can gain his confidence. It is the start of the bonding process, and you will find that kindness and patience are always rewarded in this situation.

The best place to locate the crate is in a sectioned-off area in the kitchen or in a warm utility room. Your puppy will feel safe and secure but he can still see what is going on around him. When it is time for bed, put your puppy in his crate with some safe toys and a warm water bottle, making sure it is well covered. It

is also a good idea to place some newspaper or a puppy training pad in the front half of the crate so your puppy can use it during the night if he needs to relieve himself.

If there is no activity going on around him, he should settle. If he whimpers to begin with, leave him, as he will probably give up and go to sleep. It is best not to leave him to get really stressed so, if needs be, give him a cuddle to reassure him that all is well. Let him play for a while and repeat the same routine, this time leaving him with a chew or treat. Try not to give in too quickly if he complains again; these clever, little Miniature Schnauzers do catch on very quickly, and they will soon learn they can get attention on demand.

Given the right training, I am sure your new Miniature Schnauzer puppy will settle in well – but I am equally sure that when he is older, he will be sleeping on your bed!

## HOUSE TRAINING

If you can section off a small area alongside the cage, he will keep his bed clean and overnight will use the puppy paper to soil if needed. Ask the breeder for some of the litter's soiled paper, a small piece with the scent on, as this will encourage the pup to go in the place of your choice. In the daytime you can let the puppy outside the pen and put the paper by the outside door – this, again, is encouragement to go in the right place. After a few days put the paper outside and, very soon,

**It is inevitable that your puppy will miss the company of his littermates for the first few nights.**

he will be going into the garden himself. Miniature Schnauzers are naturally clean dogs and, given the chance, will not make a mess.

Small puppies do need to spend pennies quite often and at regular intervals. Take your puppy out at the following times:

- First thing in the morning
- After eating
- After a play session
- On waking up from a snooze
- Last thing at night.

Your puppy should be taken out at least every two hours – more often if you can manage it – for the first couple of weeks.

### TOILETING IN THE GARDEN.

The first time you take your Miniature Schnauzer to the garden for toileting, take him on a lead or carry him to the area you would prefer him to use as his toilet. Once he has made his mark in that area he will almost always use that spot of his own choice. You will have to wait until he performs and then praise him well and give him a treat.

Miniature Schnauzers are quick to learn and, if you stick to a routine, your puppy will soon understand what is required.

### WHEN ACCIDENTS HAPPEN

The Miniature Schnauzer is naturally a very clean little dog, and will get most upset if he has an 'accident' in the house. Make sure you are aware of what your puppy is trying to tell you, as it is unlikely he would do this on purpose.

If your puppy makes a mistake,

# THE SCHNAUZER SHUFFLE

When your puppy has settled in and is getting more active around the house, care must be taken not to step on him, as it is easily done. Slippers or stocking feet are best, and if you shuffle rather than step, it will be less damaging to tiny legs. Your puppy will very soon learn that feet are not really the best things to play with.

**If you take your puppy out at regular intervals, he will soon learn what is required.**

## HANDLING
It is important to accustom your puppy to being handled from an early age.

To begin with, your puppy must get used to being on a table.

Run your hand along the length of his body, going to the tip of his tail.

Pick up each paw in turn.

Part his lips to inspect teeth and gums

Check the ears are clean and smell fresh.

clean up with a special solution, available from pet stores, that takes away the odour. By doing this you will lessen the chance of him using the same spot again. Do not reprimand your puppy, as it will only make him withdrawn and confused. In nearly every case, you can blame yourself for lack of vigilance.

## HANDLING AND GROOMING

Most dogs and puppies that are fed a healthy diet have good, strong teeth. Keep a check on your puppy and make sure he loses all his baby teeth, as sometimes the adult teeth come through quickly and will not push the baby teeth out. You may have to get your vet to have a look to see if all is going well.

When your puppy has his new set of teeth, it is a good idea to give him something to chew on. To help clean his teeth, some chews have a cleaning agent in them. Chewing is also a good exercise to strengthen the jaw.

Rawhide is a good toy and Kongs (with some treats inside) are a great way to keep your puppy occupied.

### WEARING A COLLAR

When your puppy is 10-12 weeks old, it is a good time to get him used to a collar. You can start by using a cat collar, which is small in size and elasticated, slipping off easily if your puppy gets caught up on anything. This is only as an introduction to wearing a collar full-time, but your pup will get used to feeling something around the neck. The collar must only be

**The Miniature Schnauzer is very adaptable, but an older dog will need time to settle into a new home.**

worn for short periods and should never be left on when your puppy is confined in his crate.

When your puppy is ignoring his collar, you can swap to a nylon, adjustable puppy collar, which will be suitable for lead training.

*For information on training and socialisation, see Chapter Six.*

### REHOMING AN OLDER DOG

If you are taking on an older dog, do not make the mistake of thinking that he comes

'readymade' and will fit into your home without any effort. An older dog may be familiar with a home environment, and he may well be house trained, but changing homes is potentially very traumatic and he is likely to feel unsettled to begin with.

Make sure you spend time with the older dog, introducing him to his new home and family, just as you would do with a puppy. Be patient with him and give lots of reassurance and he will soon relax and appreciate his new home.

# THE BEST OF CARE

Now a Miniature Schnauzer has come into your life, you will have to care for him – feeding him, grooming him, and exercising him – as you are now responsible for all his needs.

## UNDERSTANDING NUTRITION

All animals need a balanced diet in order to remain healthy and the Miniature Schnauzer is no exception. We are fortunate, nowadays, that there are very good commercial dog foods available and we have a wide choice in supermarkets and pet shops.

Before choosing a diet to suit your Miniature Schnauzer, it is important to know what essential ingredients he requires in order to remain healthy.

### PROTEIN
Proteins are the building blocks in a dog's nutrition. A Miniature Schnauzer will need a certain level of protein in his diet in order to maintain all aspects of growth and development and to support a healthy immune system. In addition, protein is burned as calories and is converted to – and stored as – fat. Proteins are found in eggs, meat and fish.

### CARBOHYDRATES
Carbohydrates provide a quick energy source. You will find high carbohydrate levels in all grains, including rice, wheat, corn, barley and oats.

Historically, canines would have had very little carbohydrate in their diet. However, commercial dog foods are often high in carbohydrate, but this seems to be tolerated well.

### FATS
Fats have had some bad press and yet they are absolutely vital for a Miniature Schnauzer to remain in tip-top condition. Fats are another energy source and they are vital for growth and development, wound healing, plus a healthy skin and coat. Dog food contains many types of fat, such as meat fats (lard), fish oils or vegetable oils.

### VITAMINS AND MINERALS
Both vitamins and minerals are required in a balanced diet. For example, vitamin B boosts the immune system, and a balance of calcium and phosphorus are required to build strong bones and cartilage. Commercial diets are formulated with the correct ratios of minerals and vitamins, and so there is no need to add supplements.

**You need to find a diet to suit your dog's age and lifestyle.**

## WATER

Fresh drinking water is essential in the diet. You will need to keep a regular check on the water you provide. Because Miniature Schnauzers have beards, which they tend to drag through all sorts of disgusting matter, you will find that the water will become dirty very quickly.

## CHOOSING A DIET

The Miniature Schnauzer is a no-nonsense breed, and will thrive on most types of diet, providing it is of a suitably high quality. Most Miniatures have a fairly robust digestive system and rarely suffer with gastro-intestinal issues.

If you have bought your puppy from a reputable breeder then you will often be given a full feeding regime, taking account of what the puppy has been reared on. It may well be worth sticking to this regime because it is likely that, after many years experience, the breeder has found what works best for their dogs.

## COMPLETE

A complete dog food, which comes in the form of a dry kibble, is probably the easiest diet to feed. Manufacturers now produce different diets for your dog's life stages as he moves from Puppy through to Junior, Adult and

Senior. There are diets for pregnant and lactating bitches, and there also diets that are formulated to help with specific health issues. Some manufacturers even produce a Miniature Schnauzer breed-specific food.

In many ways, complete diets take the guesswork out of feeding, and most dogs seem to thrive on them. However, as mentioned before, your Miniature Schnauzer needs a good-quality diet, so do not go for the cheapest option. There can be major differences in ingredients from one manufacturer to the next, so carefully check the list of

**A complete diet does not need to be supplemented.**

**Most dogs find canned food highly appetising.**

**A homemade diet needs to be carefully balanced to make sure your Mini receives the nutrients he needs in the correct proportions.**

ingredients printed on the packaging.

The kibble in most complete diets is shaped so that there is less tartar build-up on the teeth. This is important in the Miniature Schnauzer because they are prone to dental disease.

The advantage of complete food is that it is specially formulated to cater for all your dog's needs, so there is no need to add supplements. In fact, it is advisable not to do this or you risk upsetting the nutritional balance.

### CANNED
If you have a fussy eater, you may opt for canned food or pouches, which are often more palatable than kibble. You do need to watch for dental disease, though, and you will need to take your dog to the vet for regular dental check-ups, maybe at vaccination time.

This type of food also has a high moisture content, so you need to check the ingredients to ensure

your Miniature Schnauzer is getting all the essential nutrients in the correct proportions.

### HOMEMADE
If a commercial diet is not for you, then you could always look towards a more natural approach, feeding fresh raw fish, meaty bones, raw mince and pureed vegetables, along with brewer's yeast and flaxseed oil. This method takes more work and you need to ensure that your dog is getting a balanced diet – particularly the phosphorus (meat) and calcium (bones) ratio. However, the extra effort is rewarded with cleaner teeth, resulting in less dental disease and fresher breath. You will also find that your dog's stools will be smaller and firmer.

### FEEDING A PUPPY
If you have purchased your Miniature Schnauzer as an eight-week-old puppy, then your little

bundle will require four feeds, evenly spaced throughout the day. He will need breakfast, lunch, dinner and a bedtime meal. Obviously, you can time the meals to suit your own convenience, but try to keep to a routine, as they will help your puppy to settle – and will also hasten the house-training process. Your puppy only has a small stomach at this stage, so little and often is best. The breeder should give you detailed information on how much to feed, which will change as your puppy grows and as you reduce the number of meals he is getting.

By the time your puppy is about four months of age, you can reduce the number of meals to three per day, and then, when he is six months old, he can go down to two meals.

### ADULT FEEDING
As your puppy matures, it is your choice whether you continue to

**It is your job to keep your Mini fit and active.**

feed two meals per day or whether you drop further to one meal per day. The age at which you drop to one meal per day would depend on your dog's weight and maturity, but it is usually when a Miniature Schnauzer is around 12 months of age.

Some owners advocate free feeding, where food is always available and the dog chooses when to eat and how much he eats at any one time. Because Miniature Schnauzers are often greedy, this could result in obesity. This method does not really help with dogs that are reluctant to eat, either, as they tend to eat more if a certain amount of food is given at specific times during the day.

## DANGERS OF OBESITY
As a rule, Miniature Schnauzers are the dustbins of the dog world. They will eat anything and

everything and are consequently prone to weight gain. Some puppies can be a little fussy when they are young, but these often grow up to be good eaters.

Keeping an adult Miniature Schnauzer slim can be a never-ending battle. One thing to remember is that they are only small dogs, so do not require a huge amount of food. Often an adult will keep optimum weight when being fed only two handfuls of complete food per day – and *that's it!*

You should always be able to feel your dog's ribs – if your dog resembles a table top when viewed from above, then he is too fat. Obesity can cause difficulty in breathing; your dog will exercise less and be unable to tolerate heat. From a health point of view, being overweight will not only cause cardiovascular problems, but you will also put unnecessary

strain on your Mini's joints and ligaments.

## TREATS
Treats can be used as an excellent tool to train your Miniature Schnauzer. You can give any of the available commercial dog treats. Always supervise when you give hard, chewy treats, as there is a danger of choking.

## BEWARE!
Your Miniature Schnauzer will eat everything you put before him – and anything else he can find along the way. However, you need to be aware that some foods that are fine for us, can be toxic to dogs. These include chocolate, grapes and raisins. For more detailed information, research on the internet.

## COAT CARE
Whether you buy a Miniature

Schnauzer as a pet or as a show dog, there is considerable effort required to keep your dog looking smart. As a general rule, most pet Miniature Schnauzers are taken to the grooming parlour every six weeks, and in between the owners keep them maintained by regular bathing, brushing and nail clipping.

If you are thinking of showing your beloved Mini, then this is where the hard work begins. However, there is no need to feel daunted; it really is not that bad if you keep on top of it and get into a routine.

### PUPPY GROOMING

It is vitally important that your puppy gets used to being groomed from an early age. Any good breeder will have given you a head start, by brushing the puppy regularly and clipping around his rear end. Make you sure have the correct tools to carry on with this.

You will need the following:

- A small, soft slicker brush for the leg furnishings, skirt and beard. This can also be used to gently brush the hair of the body coat, although this hair rarely gets long enough to cause a problem if the dog is groomed.
- A small, fine comb for the eyebrows.

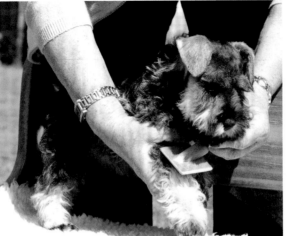
**A small slicker brush can be used for the leg furnishings and the body coat.**

- A large metal comb for the furnishings and beard.
- A pair of thinning scissors to tease out knots and to blend the clipped areas to the stripped coat.

The easiest way to groom your puppy is to lay him on his back (on your lap) and gently start by brushing his legs and skirt. Choose a time when he is tired after an hour or so of playing. Get him used to all the fiddly bits, such as under his elbows, and then brush his eyebrows and beard. Be gentle: if he has a knot, do not pull it out; gently tease with a pair of scissors.

### ADULT GROOMING

Regardless of whether you have a pet dog or a show dog, you should set aside a time each week to work on your dog. This is essential for the show dog, but a

pet dog also needs regular care. A grooming session provides an opportunity to keep a close check on your Miniature Schnauzer so you can spot any signs of trouble – lumps, bumps, or sore places – at an early stage.

### THE COAT

The coat on a Miniature Schnauzer consists of two types of hair: a soft, downy undercoat and a harsh wire top coat. In terms of routine grooming, the coat has to be kept free from dirt and other debris, as well as free from tangles and mats. Grooming is also beneficial in that it aids circulation and acts as a massage.

If you are not planning to show your dog, you will not need a full range of grooming equipment, but it is important to invest in some reasonable gear, as you will be using it on a weekly basis throughout your dog's life.

The best type of brush to buy is a slicker brush, which has small, wire bristles. When choosing a slicker brush, run your hand against the wire bristles and if it feels too harsh, choose a softer one. These tend to pull out less hair when brushing and are gentler on the skin. Choose a comb with two types of tooth-width for versatility; the wider tooth is great for fluffing the furnishings and the narrower tooth is needed for more intricate

## ROUTINE GROOMING

You will need to brush an adult's coat on a daily basis.

Debris collects in the beard so this needs to be combed through.

Tidy up the eyebrows.

Work down the chest.

Pay attention to the leg furnishings.

areas, such as the eyebrows.

If you plan to take your pet Miniature Schnauzer to a professional groomer for the clipping and scissoring work, then you will still have to maintain the coat in between times.

### DAILY

Brush your dog daily. The easiest way to do this is to lay the dog upside down on your lap and brush the skirt, legs, beard and eyebrows. If you started this regime from a young age, you should have no problem once your dog matures. Some Miniature Schnauzers will mat easily, so you need to make sure that you remove all knots on a daily basis. Gently tease the knots out with a pair of scissors or thinning scissors. Do *not* pull them out with your comb. The best way to test for any mats is to comb your dog after you have brushed him thoroughly. If your comb does not run through the hair easily, you have a knot that will need to be removed.

**Teeth:** It is vitally important that your Miniature Schnauzer's teeth are kept clean and plaque-free. To maintain good dental hygiene, get into a routine of brushing your dog's teeth on a daily basis with an enzymatic toothpaste or gel that is specially formulated for dogs.

### WEEKLY

Shampoo and condition your Miniature Schnauzer's legs and beard on a weekly basis. There is no need to bath the body, as the coat is short here, unless your dog has found something smelly to roll

in. For a super finish, dry your Mini with a hair dryer on a moderate heat. For the beard, use either a tear-free dog or baby shampoo and try not to go too close to the eye.

If you have a show dog, refrain from bathing him all over too often, as it will spoil the harsh texture of the topcoat. After shampooing, use a really good conditioner to keep the leg hair and beard from breaking.

Regardless of whether you have a show dog or a pet dog, your Miniature Schnauzer will need to have his legs and skirt scissored. Your groomer will either do this for you at your regular grooming visits or you could have a go yourself. The procedure is the same for a show dog or a pet (see page 72).

**Nails:** Nails grow surprising quickly. Every time you bath your Miniature Schnauzer, check his nail length. If they are long, either cut them using nail clippers or grind them with a nail grinder.

**Ears:** Periodically, your Miniature Schnauzer will need the hair removed from the inside of his ears. This helps to prevent any infections. Check the inside of your Miniature Schnauzer's ears weekly. If there is a lot of hair growing from inside the ear canal, either get your groomer to remove it or remove it yourself with your finger

and thumb or with a pair of tweezers. It is best to use an ear powder, as this aids the removal and causes less distress. If you see a brown waxy residue, your dog may have ear mites or a fungal infection. It is worth a trip to the vet to get this checked out.

### CLIPPING

On average, a pet Miniature Schnauzer will need to have the body clipped every six weeks. This involves clipping the top of the head, cheeks, throat, chest, and the body (clipping down to the elbows, skirt and second thigh).

**To maintain his smart appearance, a pet dog will need clipping every six weeks.**

Instead of clipping, show dogs are hand-stripped. So why not strip a pet? The answer is because it involves a lot of hard work and you need to tweak it constantly. This is an ongoing job that most pet owners find too labour intensive.

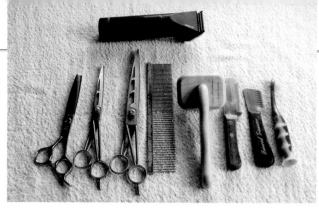

GROOMING EQUIPMENT: Top row: Cordless clippers with adjustable blades.
Bottom row, from the left: Thinning scissors; Smaller pair of scissors for trimming around ears, feet etc.; Larger pair of scissors for all furnishings; Comb; Slicker brush; Fine stripping knife for scraping out the undercoat; Coarse stripping knife for maintaining the harsh top coat; Toothbrush.

### FINDING A GOOD GROOMER

The best way to find a groomer for your Miniature Schnauzer is to contact your nearest Miniature Schnauzer Breed Club. They will have a database of breeders that groom in your area and, because they often show Minis themselves, they will present your dog in the correct trim.

### THE SHOW DOG

If you are showing your Miniature Schnauzer you will need some basic tools to get started. You can buy these items (or similar) at most good pet stores or online. Buying good-quality grooming items is not for the faint hearted when it comes to cost, but good equipment will last you a lifetime.

### CLIPPERS

There are many different types of clipper on the market with various price tags. As with all consumables, you get what you pay for. Depending on your preference the different types of clipper include the choice of:

**Corded or cordless:** Cordless clippers are lighter to handle and often less noisy, but they are not as robust and can break easily if dropped. These are good if you only have one or two dogs and they are brilliant on puppies. If you plan on grooming a lot of dogs, then you may opt for mains-driven clippers, which are more hard-wearing.

**Detachable or adjustable blades:** Detachable blades can be easily sharpened, but you have to buy several different sizes in order to cope with the demands of a Miniature. The sizes you will need are as follows:

- Size 30: This will clip the hair very short, so you will use this on the cheeks, throat and ears.
- Size 10: A slightly longer blade, which is useful for the rear and the belly. In a pet Miniature Schnauzer, this size is often used on the body as well, if a short jacket is required.
- Size 7F: This is used on a pet

for the body area if a longer coat is required - for example, in the winter months.

### SCISSORS

Of all the things that you will need in your grooming kit, scissors are one of the most important items, and should be where you skimp the least. *Buy good quality.* Cheaper scissors will not cut the hair as well and will dull in sharpness much sooner.

You will need a smaller pair for trimming around the ears and feet, a long pair – around 8.5 inches (21 cms) – for scissoring the legs, plus a pair of thinning scissors for blending clipped and scissored areas.

### STRIPPING KNIVES

You will need two types of stripping knife – one medium/fine blade, which is used to scrape out the undercoat, and one coarse blade to strip out the longer harsh hair.

### HAND-STRIPPING

The coat of a Miniature Schnauzer must be hand-stripped in order to obtain the required harsh jacket that the Breed Standard asks for. All areas are stripped except for the cheeks, throat, ears, tummy and rear, which are clippered. The legs, eyebrows and beard are scissored.

It is best to start hand-stripping

## HAND-STRIPPING

**Drag the fine tooth stripping knife through the jacket to scrape out the undercoat**

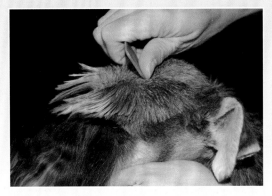

**To take out the harsh hair use the coarse tooth stripping knife. Lift the hair with the thumb and then use the knife-edge to pull the hair out by the root. Care must be taken to ensure that the hair is not cut by the knife. You can also remove this hair by pulling with your finger and thumb.**

**The top of the head will also need stripping.**

the coat when your puppy is around 10 weeks old. Start with a fine blade and gently scrape all the soft undercoat out. Your puppy will probably not like this very much, so you need to be firm with him, but remember to reward him at frequent intervals.

Once all the soft undercoat is out, take out the remaining long, coarse hairs by pulling them between your finger and thumb or using a coarse stripping knife. Whether this stage takes an afternoon or several sessions will depend on your puppy's age and

coat type.

After a month or so, you should start to see the new coat coming through. If your puppy has quite a lot of undercoat then you will need to keep on top of this throughout – scraping, scraping, scraping. A profuse amount of undercoat will stop any coarse hair growth. Some types of undercoat can be very stubborn to pull out – in this case use a grooming or stripping powder to aid in the removal.

Once the puppy coat is out, you start with your first adult coat. You will then have a choice as to how you keep the coat throughout the dog's adult life: you can either 'roll the coat' or 'blanket strip'.

### THE ROLLED COAT

In order to keep a Schnauzer in coat throughout the year – so that he does not have periods of looking rather patchy – the best method is to roll the coat. This is a process where you lightly strip the jacket once a week, or once every two weeks depending on the thickness for each individual dog. Strip approximately a handful of hair each time so that you end up with a coat that consists of lots of different lengths.

I begin rolling the jacket as soon as a new coat starts to break through and is fairly close to the skin. It is the quality of the coat that will decide whether this is done with the first adult coat, at around five to six months, or whether to wait for the coat after this. You need a thick, harsh jacket in order to start this process. If you have a lot of fluff and soft undercoat, or a coat that is slow growing, rolling the coat will not work for you. I might only take a small handful out each week, but this just starts the ball rolling.

When you first start rolling the jacket, there will be a stage when you will have a somewhat moth-eaten look – often around eight weeks in. This is perfectly normal and does not tend to last too long – usually just a couple of weeks. It is a case of waiting for the new coat underneath to break through.

### BLANKET/SECTION STRIPPING

Blanket or section stripping is where the whole coat is taken out at the same time or in sections. The dog is stripped to its underwear; he is pretty much bald, with just a small amount of undercoat left. It takes from 10-12 weeks for a coat to grow from scratch, so if you use this method, you need to ensure that you get the timing right for each show. This method is better if your dog has a poorer/sparser coat.

Another advantage of this method is that you can take out sections of the coat at different time periods, in order to hide your dog's flaws. For example, if your dog has a slightly low-set tail or is ewe-necked, then by stripping the area just before the tail or at the base of the neck first, you will get more coat growth in these sections. This produces longer hair length, which gives an illusion that the topline is good or that the dog has a lovely arched neck. You can still disguise faults such as this with a rolled jacket, but it is easier with this method.

With both methods you need to look at your dog and strip

accordingly. Never strip the topline without looking at the dog's reflection in a mirror and assessing which bits need to come off and what needs to stay. As a general rule, the hair at the base of the neck, just behind the shoulder and at the base of the tail, always needs to be slightly fuller to give that perfect neckline, topline and tailset.

### CLIPPING

Clip the cheeks, tummy and rear end. There is no reason to strip this area unless you have an issue with coat colour. The ears can be either stripped and then clipped or clipped only. You would choose to strip the ears first if you need to keep the colour uniform – for example, in a pure black dog. Sometimes a black and silver that has excessively light ears or a pepper and salt that has very dark or light ears will have their ears stripped first, in order for the colour to blend in with the head.

### SCISSORING

Scissoring is where the furnishings are sculpted to achieve the flawless columns on the front legs and the shapely rear. It really does not matter where you start, but most people begin with the front legs (see page 72), then move on to the hind legs and skirt (see page 73), with the head being done either first or last.

### THE TAIL

The tail is stripped in the show dog or clipped on a pet.

## CLIPPING

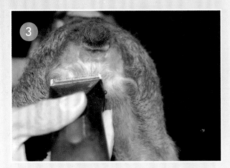

1, 2, 3: Clip the ears, cheeks, tummy and rear end. When clipping the ears ensure that you clip towards the ear edge as it is very easy to nick this sensitive area, which can result in a lot of bleeding.

## SCISSORING: EARS AND FEET

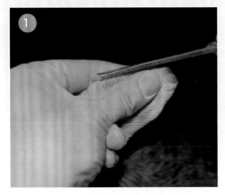

4: After using the clippers on the ears, use your small scissors to take off the remaining hair around the edge of the ear.

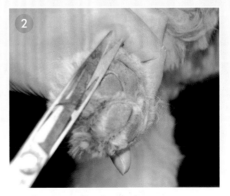

5: Using a small pair of scissors, trim around the bottom of the feet.

## SCISSORING: THE BODY

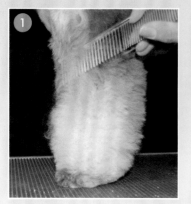

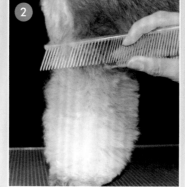

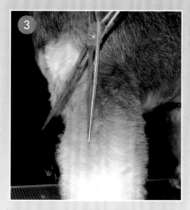

**1, 2:** Comb the furnishings using a flicking-up motion to fluff them and prepare for scissoring.

**3, 4, 5, 6:** Cut the front legs into columns by scissoring in straight lines down the leg.

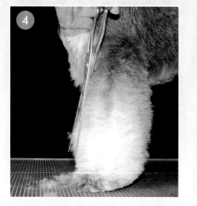

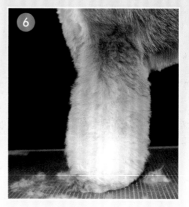

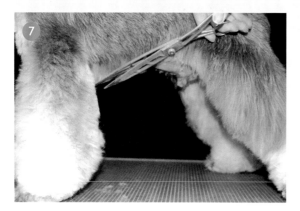

**7:** Cut the skirt in a straight line following the line of the ribcage with a slight 'tuck up'.

8, 9, 10, 11: Follow the line of the hind leg when scissoring at the front of the leg. With your comb, flick the hair at the hock out, then cut a line at a slight angle back towards the foot. Trim any excess hair at the back of the hind leg (up towards the tail), taking the natural line of the hind limb.

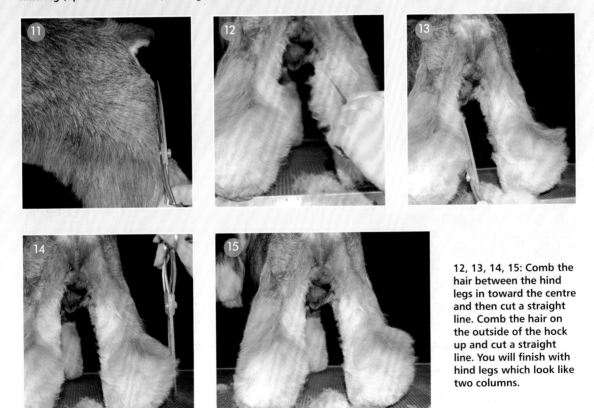

12, 13, 14, 15: Comb the hair between the hind legs in toward the centre and then cut a straight line. Comb the hair on the outside of the hock up and cut a straight line. You will finish with hind legs which look like two columns.

## SCISSORING: THE HEAD

16, 17, 18: Comb the eyebrows out to the side. Then cut them in a straight line, placing your scissors at the side of the nose, and aiming for the corner of the eye and flat of the cheek.

After all the hard work, the Miniature Schnauzer presents a stunning picture in the show ring. This is 'Sizzle' (Ch. ToMar's Two Thumbs Up To Zakmayo), a multi All Breed Championship Show Group Winner and a Multi BISS winner. He was Top Dog and Top Sire in 2009.

### THE BEARD

The beard is pretty much left to grow with just the ends trimmed to remove any straggly bits.

### THE FINISHED RESULT

In the show ring the standard of presentation is very high. Historically, those in the USA have been considerably better with their grooming skills than those in the UK. However, the bar has been raised in the UK and now, in order to have a certain amount of success, you need to be able to present your dog to perfection.

### EXERCISING YOUR MINIATURE SCHNAUZER

Miniature Schnauzers must be one of the most versatile breeds, as they will fit into pretty much any lifestyle. As adults they are equally at home racing around a local park or sitting on their owner's knee.

However, caution must be taken when exercising a puppy. Start off with short walks and, as the puppy matures, this can be lengthened. You will find that your puppy has short bursts of high energy and then he will collapse into a deep sleep. This sleep is important for his growth, and so the puppy should be left to rest undisturbed. When young, your main aim of exercise is to socialise your puppy, it should not be your aim to run the life out of him.

As a rule, Miniature Schnauzers are sociable little dogs. They want to make friends and play with other dogs. They were originally descended from the Standard Schnauzer, their larger cousin who was bred to guard, using this voice

**A puppy will get as much exercise as he needs playing in the garden.**

without the bite reaction. This instinct can still be quite inherent in the breed today. Therefore, if a Miniature Schnauzer is unsure or feels threatened, he is likely to bark and yet has no desire to bite. You need to be aware of this, because if your Miniature Schnauzer is not socialised with other dogs from a young age, this could result in owning a dog that will bark at anything and everything.

When exercising, remember that your Miniature Schnauzer has fluffy furnishings covering his legs and tummy. This pretty much acts as Velcro to any twigs, leaves, sticky buds, etc. that you may come into contact with on a walk. It is therefore important that you brush your dog after exercise and

ensure that there are no mats or knots formed. We are fortunate that, as a general rule, Miniature Schnauzers do not like to get dirty. They will often walk around a puddle and will rarely swim. They do, however, love the snow and will frolic in it for hours. When they return indoors, you may need to bath them, as the snow tends to ball up in the furnishings, which can cause frostbite.

### PLAYING GAMES

Miniature Schnauzers love their toys, and playing with toys provides mental stimulation as well physical exercise. Because they rarely chew, they can usually have any type of dog toy and not destroy it. However, I tend to find

**A game with a toy has the added bonus of providing mental stimulation.**

that they prefer the soft teddy-type of toy, rather than a hard ball. Tug-of-war is one of their favourite games. They will also fetch their teddy if you throw it, but this is not the type of dog that will retrieve over and over again. After a while, your Mini will look at you, as if to say: "Well, you threw it – so you go and get it!"

The best game of all for a Miniature Schnauzer is to play fight with another dog. Minis can be quite vocal when playing, but they mean no harm.

## TRAINING FOR THE SHOW RING

In order to produce a fluent, effortless trot in the show ring, you will need to put in some extra effort. I have discovered that running your dog safely alongside you on a bike will produce the best results. You don't need to go far, just a hundred yards or so. This helps to achieve a good rhythm and teaches your dog to move in a straight line. The aim of this exercise is not to build up the muscles to resemble a turkey

drumstick, but to teach good balance while on the move.

## GETTING OLDER

Miniature Schnauzers often live to around 14 years old, with 12 years being the average lifespan (according to the Kennel Club Breed Health Survey). They can remain fairly fit and full of life right to the end. However, as is often the case, in the final year or two, your golden oldie will start to slow up. He will still want to go on his jaunt around the park and woe betide if you even tried

Be aware of the changing needs of your Miniature Schnauzer as he grows older.

leaving him at home. But a leisurely stroll rather than a mad dash is likely to be the order of the day.

As Miniature Schnauzers age, you need to ensure, particularly in the later years, that the coat is kept free of mats and tangles. As with all species, their skin gets thinner with age, meaning that it becomes more sensitive to brushing and combing. Visiting the grooming parlour regularly and keeping the coat short is an absolute must.

There is rarely a need to change the diet of your old friend, unless recommended by your vet.

## LETTING GO

Seeing your beloved pet grow old, and watching his health deteriorate, is possibly one of the hardest things that you will have to come to terms with. You will know when it is the right time to let go, when your dog is suffering or when their quality of life is at a minimum. However, this does not make the decision any easier. But for the wellbeing of your Mini, it is a decision that you owe to your dog.

People deal with loss in different ways. Whether you decide to have a memorial, such as a casket or planting a tree, is personal to each of us. Some people cannot bear a house without a dog and will buy a new puppy immediately; others prefer to wait until the initial pain has subsided. You will never forget your old boy and a new puppy will never take his place – but it can fill a void, and you will come to love and value your new Mini in his own right.

# SOCIALISATION AND TRAINING

## Chapter 6

When you decided to bring a Miniature Schnauzer into your life, you probably had dreams of how it was going to be: long walks together, cosy evenings with a Miniature lying devotedly at your feet, and, whenever you returned home, there would always be a special welcome waiting for you.

There is no doubt that you can achieve all this – and much more – with a Miniature Schnauzer, but like anything that is worth having, you must be prepared to put in the work. A Miniature, regardless of whether he is a puppy or an adult, does not come ready trained, understanding exactly what you want and fitting perfectly into your lifestyle. A Miniature Schnauzer has to learn his place in your family and he must discover what is acceptable behaviour.

We have a great starting point in that the breed has an outstanding temperament. He is adaptable and always ready and willing to co-operate with his human family. He is also highly intelligent. Given the chance he will run circles round you, so you must be on your mettle to bring out the best in him.

### THE FAMILY PACK
Dogs have been domesticated for some 14,000 years, but luckily for us, they have inherited and retained behaviour from their distant ancestor – the wolf. A Miniature Schnauzer may never have lived in the wild, but he is born with the survival skills and the mentality of a meat-eating predator who hunts in a pack. A wolf living in a pack owes its existence to mutual co-operation and an acceptance of a hierarchy, as this ensures both food and protection. A domesticated dog living in a family pack has exactly the same outlook. He wants food, companionship and leadership – and it is your job to provide for these needs.

### YOUR ROLE
Theories about dog behaviour and methods of training go in and out of fashion, but in reality, nothing has changed from the day when wolves ventured in from the wild to join the family circle. The wolf (and equally the dog) accepts a subservient place in the family pack in return for food and protection. In a dog's eyes, you are his leader and he relies on you to make all the important decisions. This does not mean that you have to act like a dictator or a bully. You are accepted as a leader, without argument, as long as you have the right credentials.

The first part of the job is easy. You are the provider and you are therefore respected because you supply food. In a Miniature Schnauzer's eyes, you must be the ultimate hunter, because a day never goes by when you cannot find food. The second part of the leader's job description is straightforward, but for some reason we find it hard to achieve. In order for a dog to accept his place in the family pack, he must respect his leader as the decision-maker. A low-ranking pack animal does not question authority; he is perfectly happy to see someone else shoulder the responsibility. Problems will only arise if you cut a poor figure as leader and the dog feels he should mount a challenge for the top-ranking role.

## HOW TO BE A GOOD LEADER

There are a number of guidelines to follow to establish yourself in the role of leader in a way that your Miniature Schnauzer understands and respects. If you have a puppy, you may think you don't have to take this on board for a few months, but that would be a big mistake. With a Miniature Schnauzer it is absolutely essential to start as you mean to go on. This is a breed

**Have you got what it takes to be a firm, fair and consistent leader?**

that is clever enough to work things out and will decide whether to co-operate or not. The behaviour he learns as a puppy will continue throughout his adult life, which means that undesirable behaviour can be difficult to rectify.

When your Miniature Schnauzer first arrives in his new home, follow these guidelines:

• **Keep it simple:** Decide on the rules you want your Miniature Schnauzer to obey and always make it 100 per cent clear what is acceptable, and what is unacceptable, behaviour.

• **Be consistent:** If you are not consistent about enforcing rules, how can you expect your Miniature Schnauzer to take

you seriously? There is nothing worse than allowing your Miniature to jump on the sofa one moment and then scolding him the next time he does it because he is muddy. As far as the Miniature Schnauzer is concerned, he may as well try it on because he can't predict your reaction. Bear in mind, inconsistency leads to insecurity.

• **Get your timing right:** If you are rewarding your Miniature Schnauzer and equally if you are reprimanding him, you must respond within one to two seconds otherwise the dog will not link his behaviour with your reaction.

• **Read your dog's body language:** Find out how to read body language and facial expressions (see page 81) so that you understand your Miniature Schnauzer's feelings and intentions.

• **Be aware of your own body language:** You can help your dog to learn by using your body language to communicate with him. For example, if you want your dog to come to you, open your arms out and look inviting. If you want your dog to stay, use a hand signal (palm flat, facing the dog) so you are effectively 'blocking' his advance.

- **Tone of voice:** Dogs do not speak English; they learn by associating a word with the required action. However, they are very receptive to tone of voice, so you can use your voice to praise him or to correct undesirable behaviour. If you are pleased with your Miniature Schnauzer, praise him to the skies in a warm, happy voice. If you want to stop him raiding the bin, use a deep, stern voice when you say, "No".

- **Give one command only:** If you keep repeating a command, or keeping changing it, your Miniature Schnauzer will think you are babbling and will probably ignore you. If your Miniature does not respond the first time you ask, make it simple by using a treat to lure him into position and then you can reward him for a correct response.

- **Daily reminders:** A young, excitable Miniature Schnauzer is apt to forget his manners from time to time and an adolescent dog may attempt to challenge your authority (see page 105). Rather than coming down on your Miniature like a ton of bricks when he does something wrong, try to prevent bad manners by daily reminders of good manners. For example:
  i. Do not let your dog barge ahead of you when you are going through a door.
  ii. Do not let him leap out of the car the moment you open the door (which could be potentially lethal, as well as being disrespectful).

**Your Miniature Schnauzer will learn from your body language.**

  iii. Do not let him eat from your hand when you are at the table.
  iv. Do not let him 'win' a toy at the end of a play session and then make off with it. You 'own' his toys and you 'allow' him to play with them. Your Miniature Schnauzer must learn to give up a toy when you ask.

## UNDERSTANDING YOUR MINIATURE SCHNAUZER

Body language is an important means of communication between dogs, which they use to make friends, to assert status and to avoid conflict. It is important to get on your dog's wavelength by understanding his body language and reading his facial expressions.

- A positive body posture and a wagging tail indicate a happy, confident dog.
- A crouched body posture with ears back and tail down show that a dog is being submissive. A dog may do this when he is being told off or if a more assertive dog approaches him.
- A bold dog will stand tall, looking strong and alert. His ears will be forward and his tail will be held high.
- A dog who raises his hackles (lifting the fur along his topline) is trying to look as scary as possible.
- A playful dog will go down on his front legs while standing on his hind legs in a bow position.

You can learn a lot by watching two dogs meet. The Miniature Schnauzer is confident and ready to greet the other dog. However, the other dog is tense because he is not sure that he understands the Mini's intentions.

This friendly invitation says: "I'm no threat, let's play."

- A dominant, aggressive dog will meet other dogs with a hard stare. If he is challenged, he may bare his teeth and growl and the corners of his mouth will be drawn forward. His ears will be forward and he will appear tense in every muscle.
- A nervous dog will often show aggressive behaviour as a means of self-protection. If threatened, this dog will lower his head and flatten his ears. The corners of his mouth may be drawn back and he may bark or whine.
- Some Miniature Schnauzers are 'smilers', curling up their top lip and showing their teeth when they greet people. This should never be confused with a snarl, which would be accompanied by the upright posture of a dominant dog. A smiling dog will have a low body posture and a wagging tail; he is being submissive and

it is a greeting that is often used when low-ranking animals greet high-ranking animals in a pack.

- With a Miniature Schnauzer, the ears do the talking: when they are pricked, he is alert and interested; when they are relaxed, he is content; when they are pinned back, he is worried; and there are times when a Miniature Schnauzer will almost turn his ears inside out, which is usually a gesture of disapproval.
- A raised paw is typical of the Miniature Schnauzer – he is generally asking for something, and wondering why you are being so slow to respond!

## GIVING REWARDS

Why should your Miniature Schnauzer do as you ask? If you follow the guidelines given above, your Miniature should respect your authority, but what about the time when he is playing with a new doggy friend or has found a

really enticing scent? The answer is that you must always be the most interesting, the most attractive, and the most irresistible person in your Miniature Schnauzer's eyes. It would be nice to think that you could achieve this by personality alone, but most of us need a little extra help. You need to find out what is the biggest reward for your dog. In virtually every case, a Miniature Schnauzer will be motivated to work for a food reward. Food is a big issue for a Miniature, and he will keep on working for you (or pestering you until the final crumb has gone). Miniature Schnauzers enjoy toys – many appreciate a favourite cuddly toy, but you may have to work a bit harder if you want your Miniature to work for a toy. Squeaky toys are the best type to try, as they have an added 'surprise' for the ever-alert Miniature Schnauzer. Whatever reward you use, make sure it is something that your dog really wants.

When you are teaching a dog a new exercise, you should reward your Miniature Schnauzer frequently. When he knows the exercise or command, reward him randomly so that he keeps on responding to you in a positive manner.

If your Miniature Schnauzer does something extra special, like leaving a scent and coming back to you, make sure he knows how pleased you are by giving him a handful of treats or throwing his toy a few extra times. If he gets a bonanza reward, he is more likely to come back on future occasions because you have proved to be even more rewarding than his previous activity.

A food reward works wonders with most Miniature Schnauzers.

## TOP TREATS

Some trainers grade treats depending on what they are asking the dog to do. A dog may get a low-grade treat (such as a piece of dry food) to reward good behaviour on a random basis, such as sitting when you open a door or allowing you to examine his teeth. High-grade treats (which may be cooked liver, sausage or cheese) may be reserved for training new exercises, or for use in the park when you want a really good recall, for example.

Whatever type of treat you use, you should remember to subtract it from your Miniature Schnauzer's daily food ration. Miniatures love their food and it does not take many extra treats for them to pile on the pounds.

You may have a dog that works better for a toy.

Fat dogs are lethargic, prone to health problems and will almost certainly have a shorter life expectancy, so reward your Miniature Schnauzer but always keep a check on his figure!

## HOW DO DOGS LEARN?

It is not difficult to get inside your Miniature Schnauzer's head and understand how he learns, as it is not dissimilar to the way we learn. Dogs learn by conditioning: they find out that specific behaviours produce specific consequences. This is known as operant conditioning or consequence learning. Consequences have to be immediate or clearly linked to the behaviour, as a dog sees the world in terms of action and result. Dogs will quickly learn if an action has a bad consequence or a good consequence.

Dogs also learn by association. This is known as classical conditioning or association learning. It is the type of learning made famous by Pavlov's experiment with dogs. Pavlov presented dogs with food and measured their salivary response (how much they drooled). Then he rang a bell just before presenting the food. At first, the dogs did not salivate until the food was presented. But after a while they learnt that the sound of the bell meant that food was coming and so they salivated when they heard the bell. A dog needs to learn the association in order for it to have any meaning. For example, a dog that has never seen a lead before will be completely indifferent to it. A dog that has learnt that a lead means he is going for a walk will get

# THE CLICKER REVOLUTION

Karen Pryor pioneered the technique of clicker training when she was working with dolphins. It is very much a continuation of Pavlov's work and makes full use of association learning. Karen wanted to mark 'correct' behaviour at the precise moment it happened. She found it was impossible to toss a fish to a dolphin when it was in mid-air, when she wanted to reward it. Her aim was to establish a conditioned response so the dolphin knew that it had performed correctly and a reward would follow.

The solution was the clicker: a small matchbox-shaped training aid, with a metal tongue that makes a click when it is pressed. To begin with, the dolphin had to learn that a click meant that food was coming. The dolphin then learnt that it must 'earn' a click in order to get a reward. Clicker training has been used with many different animals, most particularly with dogs, and it has proved hugely successful. It is a great aid for pet owners and is also widely used by professional trainers who are training highly specialised skills.

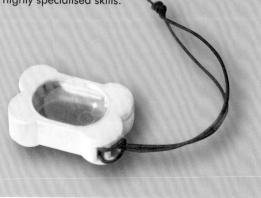

excited the second he sees the lead; he has learnt to associate a lead with a walk.

*BE POSITIVE*

The most effective method of training dogs is to use their ability to learn by consequence and to teach that the behaviour you want produces a good consequence. For example, if you ask your Miniature Schnauzer to "Sit" and reward him with a treat, he will learn that it is worth his while to sit on command because it will lead to a treat. He is far more likely to repeat the behaviour, and the behaviour will become stronger, because it results in a positive outcome. This method of training is known as positive reinforcement and it generally leads to a happy, co-operative dog that is willing to work and a handler who has fun training their dog.

The opposite approach is negative reinforcement. This is far less effective and often results in a poor relationship between dog and owner. In this method of training, you ask your Miniature Schnauzer to "Sit" and if he does not respond, you deliver a sharp yank on the training collar or push his rear to the ground. The dog learns that not responding to your command has a bad consequence and he may be less likely to ignore you in the future. However, it may well have a bad consequence for you, too. A dog that is treated in this way may associate harsh handling with the handler and become aggressive or fearful. Instead of establishing a

**If your Miniature Schnauzer is easily distracted, it may be better to start training indoors.**

pattern of willing co-operation, you are establishing a relationship built on coercion.

GETTING STARTED

As you train your Miniature Schnauzer you will develop your own techniques as you get to know what motivates him. You may decide to get involved with clicker training or you may prefer to go for a simple command-and-reward formula. It does not matter what form of training you use, as long as it is based on positive, reward-based methods.

There are a few important guidelines to bear in mind when you are training your Miniature Schnauzer:

• Find a training area that is free from distractions, particularly when you are just starting out. The Miniature Schnauzer is naturally inquisitive so it may be easier to train him indoors to begin with.

• Keep training sessions short, especially with young puppies that have very short attention spans.

• Do not train if you are in a bad

mood or if you are on a tight schedule – the training session will be doomed to failure.

- If you are using a toy as a reward, make sure it is only available when you are training. In this way it has an added value for your Miniature Schnauzer.

- If you are using food treats, make sure they are bite-size and easy to swallow; you don't want to hang about while your Miniature Schnauzer chews on his treat.

- Do not attempt to train your Miniature Schnauzer after he has eaten, or soon after returning from exercise. He will either be too full up to care about food treats or too tired to concentrate.

- When you are training, move around your allocated area so that your dog does not think that an exercise can only be performed in one place.

- If your Miniature Schnauzer is finding an exercise difficult, try not to get frustrated. Go back a step and praise him for his effort. You will probably find he is more successful when you try again at the next training session.

- If a training session is not going well – either because you are in the wrong frame of mind or the dog is not focusing – ask your Miniature Schnauzer to do something you know he can do (such as a trick he enjoys performing) and then you can reward him with a food treat or a play with his favourite toy, ending the session on a happy, positive note.

- Do not train for too long. You need to end a training session on a high, with your Miniature Schnauzer wanting more, rather than making him sour by asking too much from him.

In the exercises that follow, clicker training is introduced and followed, but all the exercises will work without the use of a clicker.

## INTRODUCING A CLICKER
This is very easy, and the intelligent Miniature Schnauzer will learn about the clicker in record time! It can be combined with attention training, which is a very useful tool and can be used on many different occasions.

- Prepare some treats and go to an area that is free from distractions. Allow your Miniature Schnauzer to wander and, when he stops to look at you, click and reward by throwing him a treat. This means he will not crowd you,

**Do not put your Miniature Schnauzer under too much pressure when you are training.**

but will go looking for the treat. Repeat a couple of times. If your Miniature is very easily distracted, you may need to start this exercise with the dog on a lead.

- After a few clicks, your Miniature Schnauzer will understand that if he hears a click, he will get a treat. He must now learn that he must 'earn' a click. This time, when your Miniature looks at you, wait a little longer before clicking and then reward him. If your Miniature is on a lead but responding well, try him off the lead.

- When your Miniature Schnauzer is working for a click and giving you his attention, you can introduce a cue or command word, such as "Watch". Repeat a few times, using the cue. You now have a Miniature Schnauzer that understands the clicker and will give you his attention when you ask him to "Watch".

**The Sit is easy to teach so is rewarding for both you and your dog.**

## TRAINING EXERCISES

A Miniature Schnauzer enjoys being busy and occupied, and so training sessions should be fun and enjoyed by both of you. The clever Miniature has great learning potential, so it is better to occupy his mind - or he will start training you!

Be creative with your training to make it varied and interesting; if you hit a problem, do not be confrontational but invent a new way of training an exercise.

The Miniature Schnauzer is an outgoing, extrovert of a dog, but he will become stressed and withdrawn if you put too much pressure on him. If your Miniature Schnauzer lies down and will not interact with you, it is a sure sign that he is not happy with proceedings. It is a gesture of surrender or 'giving in', and you will not be able to cajole him out of it. Make sure you never get to this stage when you are training.

### THE SIT

This is the easiest exercise to teach, so it is rewarding for both you and your Miniature Schnauzer.

- Choose a tasty treat and hold it just above your puppy's nose. As your Mini looks up at the treat, he will naturally go into the 'Sit'. As soon as he is in the correct position, reward him.

- Repeat the exercise and when your pup understands what you want, introduce the "Sit" command.

- You can practise the Sit exercise at mealtimes by holding out the bowl and waiting for your dog to sit. Most Miniature Schnauzers learn this one very quickly!

Lure your Mini so that he goes into the Down.

Make sure it is always rewarding for your Mini to come to you.

## THE DOWN

Work hard at this exercise because a reliable 'Down' is useful in many different situations, and an instant 'Down' can be a lifesaver.

- You can start with your dog in a 'Sit', or it is just as effective to teach it when the dog is standing. Hold a treat just below your puppy's nose and slowly lower it towards the ground. The treat acts as a lure and your puppy will follow it, first going down on his forequarters and then bringing his hindquarters down as he tries to get the treat.

- Make sure you close your fist around the treat and only reward your puppy with the treat when he is in the correct position. If your puppy is reluctant to go 'Down', you can apply gentle pressure on his shoulders to encourage him to go into the correct position.
- When your puppy is following the treat and going into position, introduce a verbal command.
- Build up this exercise over a period of time, each time waiting a little longer before giving the reward, so the puppy learns to stay in the 'Down' position.

## THE RECALL

It is never too soon to begin recall training. The Miniature Schnauzer is a busy, active dog who is endlessly curious about his surroundings. If he sees something new in the park, it can be very hard to get him back until he has conducted a full investigation. He also has a keen sense of smell, which can make him selectively 'deaf' on occasions.

Hopefully, the breeder will have already started recall training by calling the puppies in from outside and rewarding them with some treats scattered on the floor. But even if this has not been the case, you will find that a puppy arriving in his new home is highly responsive. His chief desire is to follow you and be with you. Capitalise on this from day one by getting your pup's attention and calling him to you in a bright, excited tone of voice.

- Practise in the garden. When your puppy is busy exploring, get his attention by calling his name and, as he runs towards you, introduce the verbal command "Come". Make sure you sound happy and exciting, so your puppy wants to come

to you. When he responds, give him lots of praise.
- If your puppy is slow to respond, try running away a few paces, or jumping up and down. It doesn't matter how silly you look, the key issue is to get your puppy's attention and then make yourself irresistible!
- In a dog's mind, coming when called should be regarded as the best fun because he knows he is always going to be rewarded. Never make the mistake of telling your dog off, no matter

how slow he is to respond, as you will undo all your previous hard work.
- When you call your Miniature Schnauzer to you, make sure he comes up close enough to be touched. He must understand that "Come" means that he should come right up to you, otherwise he will think that he can approach and then veer off when it suits him. As far as a Miniature is concerned, this is a great game – and one he will not tire of.
- When you are free running your

# SECRET WEAPON

You can build up a strong recall by using another form of association learning. When you are giving your Miniature Schnauzer his food, peep on a whistle. You can choose the type of signal you want to give: two short peeps or one long whistle, for example. Within a matter of days, your dog will learn that the sound of the whistle means that food is coming.

Now transfer the lesson outside. Arm yourself with some tasty treats and the whistle. Allow your Miniature Schnauzer to run free in the garden and, after a couple of minutes, use the whistle. The dog has already learnt to associate the whistle with food, so he will come towards you. Immediately reward him with a treat and lots of praise. Repeat the lesson a few times in the garden, so you are confident that your dog

is responding before trying it in the park. Make sure you always have some treats in your pocket when you go for a walk and your dog will quickly learn how rewarding it is to come to you.

dog, make sure you have his favourite toy or a pocket full of treats so you can reward him at intervals throughout the walk when you call him to you. Do not allow your dog to free run and only call him back at the end of the walk to clip on his lead. An intelligent Miniature Schnauzer will soon realise that the recall means the end of his walk and then end of fun – so who can blame him for not wanting to come back?

## TRAINING LINE

This is the equivalent of a very long lead, which you can buy at a pet store, or you can make your own with a length of rope. The training line is attached to your Miniature Schnauzer's collar and should be around 15 feet (4.5 metres) in length.

The purpose of the training line is to prevent your Miniature from disobeying you so that he never has the chance to get into bad habits. For example, when you

call your Miniature and he ignores you, you can immediately pick up the end of the training line and call him again. By picking up the line you will have attracted his attention and if you call in an excited, happy voice, your Miniature will come to you. The moment he reaches you, give him a tasty treat so he is instantly rewarded for making the 'right' decision.

The training line is very useful when your Miniature Schnauzer becomes an adolescent and is testing your leadership. When you have reinforced the correct behaviour a number of times, your dog will build up a strong recall and you will not need to use a training line.

## WALKING ON A LOOSE LEAD

This is a simple exercise but it needs to be worked on, as a Miniature Schnauzer is always keen to forge ahead and find out what is going on. In most cases, owners make the mistake of wanting to get on with the expedition rather than training the dog to walk on a lead.

In this exercise, as with all lessons that you teach your Miniature Schnauzer, you must make your training varied, offering a reward every now and then so your Miniature focuses on you and his mind is occupied with guessing when he is going to be given a treat.

- In the early stages of lead training, allow your puppy to pick his route and follow him. He will get used to the feeling of being 'attached' to you and

**The aim is for your Mini to walk on a loose lead, giving attention when required.**

has no reason to put up any resistance.

- Next, find a toy or a tasty treat and show it to your puppy. Let him follow the treat/toy for a few paces and then reward him.
- Build up the amount of time your pup will walk with you and when he is walking nicely by your side, introduce the verbal command "Heel" or "Close". Give lots of praise when your pup is in the correct position.
- When your pup is walking alongside you, keep focusing his attention on you by using his name and then rewarding him when he looks at you. If it is going well, introduce some changes of direction.
- Do not attempt to take your puppy out on the lead until you have mastered the basics at home. You need to be confident that your puppy accepts the lead and will focus his attention on you, when requested, before you face the challenge of a busy environment.
- If you are heading somewhere special, such as the park, your Miniature Schnauzer will probably try to pull because he is impatient to get there. If this happens, stop, call your dog to you and do not set off again until he is in the correct position. It may take time, but your Miniature will eventually realise that it is more productive to walk by your side than to pull ahead.

Some owners find that the Miniature Schnauzer walks better on a lead when he is wearing a harness, so this may be worth a try. Walking your Miniature on an extending lead is another option, particularly in places where it is potentially dangerous to allow him off-lead. However, it is important to bear in mind that accidents can happen when a dog is on an extending lead, if he suddenly lunges ahead and you are not quick enough to rein him in. For this reason, extending leads should never be used when you are walking in traffic.

## STAYS

This may not be the most exciting exercise, but it is one of the most useful. There are many occasions when you want your Miniature Schnauzer to stay in position, even if it is only for a few seconds. The classic example is when you want your Miniature to stay in the back of the car until you have clipped on his lead. Some trainers use the verbal command "Stay" when the dog is to stay in position for an extended period of time and "Wait" if the dog is to stay in position for a few seconds until you give the next command. Other trainers use a universal "Stay" to cover all situations. It all comes down to personal preference, and as long as you are consistent, your dog will understand the command he is given.

Watch out for the Miniature Schnauzer's brinkmanship – he will 'pretend' to stay in position, but he will go from a Sit to a

**Build up the Stay exercise in easy stages.**

Stand, or creep a couple of paces forward, as he is impatient to move on to the next thing.

- Put your puppy in a 'Sit' or a 'Down' and use a hand signal (flat palm, facing the dog) to show he is to stay in position. Step a pace away from the dog. Wait a second, step back and reward him. If you have a lively pup, you may find it easier to train this exercise on the lead, or you can try it at mealtimes and ask your Miniature Schnauzer to "Wait" a few seconds before putting his food bowl down.
- Gradually increase the distance you can leave your dog. When you return to your dog's side, praise him quietly and release him with a command, such as "OK".

- Remember to keep your body language very still when you are training this exercise and avoid eye contact with your dog. Work on this exercise over a period of time and you will build up a really reliable Stay.

Be firm and consistent with this exercise. If your Miniature Schnauzer keeps trying to break his Stay, go back to basics and reward him after a few seconds, and then build on your success.

## SOCIALISATION
While your Miniature Schnauzer is mastering basic obedience exercises, there is other, equally important work to do with him. A Miniature is not only becoming a part of your home and family, he is becoming a member of the community. He needs to be able to live in the outside world, coping calmly with every new situation that comes his way. The Miniature Schnauzer is one of the most adaptable of all breeds, but do not take this for granted and neglect his social education. It is your job to introduce your Miniature Schnauzer to as many different experiences as possible and to encourage him to behave in an appropriate manner.

In order to socialise your Miniature Schnauzer effectively, it is helpful to understand how his brain is developing and then you will get a perspective on how he sees the world.

### CANINE SOCIALISATION
*(Birth to 7 weeks)*
This is the time when a dog learns how to be a dog. By interacting with his mother and his littermates, a young pup learns about leadership and submission. He learns to read body posture so that he understands the intentions of his mother and his siblings. A puppy that is taken away from his litter too early may always have behavioural problems with other dogs, either being fearful or aggressive.

### SOCIALISATION PERIOD
*(7 to 12 weeks)*
This is the time to get cracking and introduce your Miniature Schnauzer puppy to as many different experiences as possible. This includes meeting different people, other dogs and animals, seeing new sights and hearing a

**A puppy learns his first lessons from his mother and his littermates.**

range of sounds, from the vacuum cleaner to the roar of traffic. A puppy learns very quickly and what he learns will stay with him for the rest of his life. This is the best time for a puppy to move to a new home, as he is adaptable and ready to form deep bonds.

### FEAR-IMPRINT PERIOD (8 to 11 weeks)

This occurs during the socialisation period and it can be the cause of problems if it is not handled carefully. If a pup is exposed to a frightening or painful experience, it will lead to lasting impressions. Obviously, you will attempt to avoid frightening situations, such as your pup being bullied by a mean-spirited older dog, or a firework going off, but you cannot always protect your puppy from the unexpected. If your pup has a nasty experience, the best plan is to make light of it and distract him by offering him a treat or a game. The pup will take the lead from you and will be reassured that there is nothing to worry about. If you mollycoddle him and sympathise with him, he is far more likely to retain the memory of his fear.

### SENIORITY PERIOD (12 to 16 weeks)

During this period, your Miniature Schnauzer puppy starts to cut the apron strings and becomes more independent. He will test out his status to find out who is the pack leader: him or you. Bad habits, such as play biting, which may have been seen as endearing a few weeks earlier, should be firmly

discouraged. Remember to use positive, reward-based training, but make sure your puppy knows that you are the leader and must be respected.

### SECOND FEAR-IMPRINT PERIOD (6 to 14 months)

This period is not as critical as the first fear-imprint period, but it should still be handled carefully. During this time your Miniature may appear apprehensive, or he may show fear of something familiar. You may feel as if you have taken a backwards step, but if you adopt a calm, positive manner, your Miniature Schnauzer will see that there is nothing to be frightened of. Do not make your dog confront the thing that frightens him. Simply distract his attention, and give him something else to think about, such as obeying a simple command, such as "Sit" or

"Down". This will give you the opportunity to praise and reward your dog and will help to boost his confidence.

### YOUNG ADULTHOOD AND MATURITY (1 to 4 years)

The timing of this phase depends on the size of the dog: the bigger the dog, the later it is. This period coincides with a dog's increased size and strength, mental as well as physical. Some dogs, particularly those with a dominant nature, will test your leadership again and may become aggressive towards other dogs. Firmness and continued training are essential at this time, so that your Miniature Schnauzer accepts his status in the family pack.

### IDEAS FOR SOCIALISATION

When you are socialising your Miniature, you want him to experience as many different

**A well-socialised Miniature Schnauzer will take all situations in his stride.**

situations as possible. Try out some of the following ideas, which will ensure your Miniature Schnauzer has an all-round education.

If you are taking on a rescued dog and have little knowledge of his background, it is important to work through a programme of socialisation. A young puppy soaks up new experiences like a sponge, but an older dog can still learn. If a rescued dog shows fear or apprehension, treat him in exactly the same way as you would treat a youngster who is going through the second fear-imprint period.

- Accustom your puppy to household noises, such as the vacuum cleaner, the television and the washing machine.
- Ask visitors to come to the door, wearing different types of clothing – for example, wearing a hat, a long raincoat, or carrying a stick or an umbrella.
- If you do not have children at home, make sure your Miniature Schnauzer has a chance to meet and play with them. Go to a local park and watch children in the play area. You will not be able to take your Miniature inside the play area, but he will see children playing

and will get used to their shouts of excitement.
- Attend puppy classes. These are designed for puppies between the ages of 12 to 20 weeks and give puppies a chance to play and interact together in a controlled, supervised environment. Your vet will have details of a local class.
- Take a walk around some quiet streets, such as a residential area, so your Miniature Schnauzer can get used to the sound of traffic. As he becomes more confident, progress to busier areas. Remember, your lead is like a live wire and your

# TRAINING CLUBS

Miniature Schnauzers benefit from going to training classes, as they are stimulated by a more exciting atmosphere rather than seeing training as a chore they have to do at home.

There are lots of training clubs to choose from. Your vet will probably have details of clubs in your area, or you can ask friends who have dogs if they attend a club. Alternatively, you can use the internet to find out more information. But how do you know if the club is any good?

Before you take your dog, ask if you can go to a class as an observer and find out the following:

- What experience does the instructor(s) have?

- Do they have experience with Miniature Schnauzers?
- Is the class well organised and are the dogs reasonably quiet? (A noisy class indicates an unruly atmosphere, which will not be conducive to learning.)
- Are there a number of classes to suit dogs of different ages and abilities?
- Are positive, reward-based training methods used?
- Does the club train for the Good Citizen Scheme (see page 103)?

If you are not happy with the training club, find another one. An inexperienced instructor who cannot handle a number of dogs in a confined environment can do more harm than good.

feelings will travel directly to your Miniature. Assume a calm, confident manner and your puppy will take the lead from you and have no reason to be fearful.

- Take a walk through an outdoor market or visit a car-boot sale where there will be lots of people, children in pushchairs, plus a variety of different sounds and scents.
- Go to a railway station. You don't have to get on a train if you don't need to, but your Miniature Schnauzer will have the chance to experience trains, people wheeling luggage, loudspeaker announcements and going up and down stairs and over railway bridges.
- If you live in the town, plan a trip to the country. You can enjoy a day out and provide an opportunity for your Miniature Schnauzer to see livestock, such as sheep, cattle and horses.
- One of the best places for socialising a dog is at a country fair. There will be crowds of people, livestock in pens, tractors, bouncy castles, fairground rides and food stalls.
- When your dog is over 20 weeks of age, locate a training class for adult dogs. You may find that your local training class has both puppy and adult classes.

## THE ADOLESCENT MINIATURE SCHNAUZER

It happens to every dog – and every owner. One minute you have an obedient well-behaved youngster and the next you have a boisterous adolescent who appears to have forgotten everything he ever learnt.

Every dog is an individual, so it is hard to be precise as to the exact age a Miniature Schnauzer shows adolescent behaviour but, in general, this is a relatively fast-

**An adolescent may show significant changes in behaviour.**
*Photo © istockphoto.com/David Palmer.*

maturing breed. In most cases, male Miniatures will start to change between the ages of six to eight months. A male will 'cock' his leg to mark his territory, he may show an interest in females, and he may become more assertive towards his human family and towards other dogs living in his home. A Miniature male reaches full maturity by about 20 months of age.

A female can come into season anytime from six to eight months – and she will have a season every six months or so thereafter. In the majority of cases, a female will show little change in behaviour in the run up to coming in season, and during her season. However, there are some bitches who may become lethargic and go off their food, but this is generally short-lived, and the bitch will soon return to normal and take part in all the family's activities. A female Miniature Schnauzer tends to look grown up by the time she is 12-18 months old, but she is still quite a baby. If you are planning to breed with your bitch, do not consider a mating until she is at least two years old.

Adolescence can be a trying time for both dog and owner, but it is important to retain a sense of perspective. Look at the situations from the dog's perspective and respond to uncharacteristic behaviour with firmness and consistency. Just like a teenager, an adolescent Miniature Schnauzer feels the need to flex

**The Miniature Schnauzer must learn that he cannot demand your attention.**

his muscles and challenge the status quo. But if you show that you are a strong leader (see page 90) and are quick to reward good behaviour, your Miniature will be happy to accept you as his protector and provider.

*WHEN THINGS GO WRONG*
Positive, reward-based training has proved to be the most effective method of teaching dogs, but what happens when your Miniature Schnauzer does something wrong and you need to show him that his behaviour is unacceptable? The old-fashioned school of dog training used to rely

on the powers of punishment and negative reinforcement. A dog who raided the bin, for example, was smacked. Now we have learnt that it is not only unpleasant and cruel to hit a dog, it is also ineffective. If you hit a dog for stealing, he is more than likely to see you as the bad consequence of stealing, so he may raid the bin again, but probably not when you are around. If he raided the bin some time before you discovered it, he will be even more confused by your punishment, as he will not relate your response to his 'crime'.

A more commonplace example is when a dog fails to respond to a recall in the park. When the dog eventually comes back, the owner puts the dog on the lead and goes straight home to punish the dog for his poor response. Unfortunately, the dog will have a different interpretation. He does not think: "I won't ignore a recall command because the bad consequence is the end of my play in the park." He thinks: "Coming to my owner resulted in the end of playtime – therefore coming to my owner has a bad consequence, so I won't do that again."

There are a number of strategies to tackle undesirable behaviour – and they have nothing to do with harsh handling.

**Ignoring bad behaviour:** The Miniature Schnauzer is a quick-witted dog who is very much orientated toward his family. He will focus his attention on you, and may become quite demanding if you are slow to respond. A Miniature Schnauzer may jump up at you to get attention, particularly if you keep more than one dog and he is vying with other members of the 'pack'. If you tell him off or push him down, he is perfectly happy because he has got the attention he was seeking.

In this situation, the best and most effective response is to ignore your Miniature Schnauzer. Turn your back on him, do not speak to him and avoid all eye contact. The moment he has all four feet on the ground, reward him with lots of praise, making sure he does not try to jump up again. It will not take a Miniature long to realise that jumping up is not getting the attention he wants – he only gets this when he stays on the ground. In this way you have turned the tables; your Miniature Schnauzer is no longer 'training' you to do what he wants, you are in control and he is rewarded when he behaves in the way you want.

**Stopping bad behaviour:** There are occasions when you want to call an instant halt to whatever it is your Miniature Schnauzer is doing. He may have just jumped on the sofa, or you may have caught him red-handed in the rubbish bin. He has already committed the 'crime', so your aim is to stop him and to redirect his attention. You can do this by using a deep, firm tone of voice to say "No", which will startle him,

**There are times when you want to call an instant halt to your Mini's behaviour.**

and then call him to you in a bright, happy voice. If necessary, you can attract him with a toy or a treat. The moment your Miniature Schnauzer stops the undesirable behaviour and comes towards you, you can reward his good behaviour. You can back this up by running through a couple of simple exercises, such as a 'Sit' or a 'Down' and rewarding him with treats. In this way, your Miniature focuses his attention on you and sees you as the greatest source of reward and pleasure.

In a more extreme situation, when you want to interrupt

undesirable behaviour and you know that a simple "No" will not do the trick, you can try something a little more dramatic. If you get a can and fill it with pebbles, it will make a really loud noise when you shake it or throw it. The same effect can be achieved with purpose-made training discs. The dog will be startled and stop what he is doing. Even better, the dog will not associate the unpleasant noise with you. This gives you the perfect opportunity to be the nice guy, calling the dog to you and giving him lots of praise.

## PROBLEM BEHAVIOUR

If you have trained your Miniature Schnauzer from puppyhood, survived his adolescence and established yourself as a fair and consistent leader, you will end up with a brilliant companion dog. The Miniature is a well-balanced dog, who rarely has hang-ups if he has been correctly reared and socialised.

However, it may be that you may have taken on a rescued Miniature Schnauzer that has established behavioural problems. If you are worried about your Miniature and feel out of your depth, do not delay in seeking professional help. This is readily available, usually through a referral from your vet, or you can find out additional information on the internet (see Appendices for web addresses). An animal behaviourist will have experience in tackling problem behaviour and will be able to help both you and your dog.

# TAKING CONTROL

If you have trained and socialised your Miniature Schnauzer correctly, he will know his place in the family pack and will have no desire to challenge your authority. As we have seen, adolescent males may test the boundaries, but this behaviour will not continue if you exhibit the necessary leadership skills.

If you have taken on a rescued dog who has not been trained and socialised, or if you have let your adolescent Miniature Schnauzer become over-assertive, you may find you have a problem dog who is trying to take control.

This is expressed in many different ways, which may include the following:

• Showing lack of respect for your personal space. For example, your dog will barge through doors ahead of you or jump up at you.
• Getting up on to the sofa or your favourite armchair, even though he knows this is not allowed.
• Ignoring basic obedience commands, particularly the recall.
• Showing no respect to younger members of the family, pushing amongst them and completely ignoring them.
• Male dogs may start marking (cocking their leg) in the house.
• Aggression towards people or other dogs (see page 103).

However, the most common behaviour displayed by a Miniature Schnauzer who has ideas above his station is resource guarding. This may take a number of different forms:

• Getting up on to the sofa or your favourite armchair and growling when you tell him to get back on the floor.
• Guarding his food bowl by growling when you get too close.
• Growling when anyone approaches his bed or when anyone gets too close to where he is lying.

In each of these scenarios, the Miniature Schnauzer has something he values and he aims to keep it. He does not have sufficient respect for you, his human leader, to give up what he wants and he is 'warning' you to keep away.

If you see signs of your Miniature Schnauzer behaving in this way, you must work at lowering his status so that he realises that you are the leader and he must accept your authority. Although you need to be firm, you also need to use positive training methods so that your Miniature Schnauzer is rewarded for the behaviour you want. In this way, his 'correct' behaviour will be strengthened and repeated.

The golden rule is not to become confrontational. The dog will see this as a challenge and may become even more determined not to co-operate. There are a number of steps you can take to lower your Miniature's status that are far more likely to have a successful outcome. They include:

• Go back to basics and hold daily training sessions, making sure you have some really tasty treats. Run through all the training exercises you have taught your Miniature Schnauzer. By giving him things to do, you are providing mental stimulation and you have the opportunity to make a big fuss of him and reward him when he does well. This will help to reinforce the message that you are the leader and that it is rewarding to do as you ask.

- Teach your Miniature Schnauzer something new; this can be as simple as learning a trick, such as shaking paws. Having something new to think about will keep his mind occupied and he will benefit from interacting with you. Miniature Schnauzers are natural show-offs, so give him the opportunity to perform some tricks in front of friends or family so he can enjoy the applause!

- Be 100 per cent consistent with all house rules – for example, your Miniature Schnauzer must never sit on the sofa and you must never allow him to jump up at you.

- You can reinforce your role as provider by dropping some extra treats in your Miniature Schnauzer's food bowl when he is eating. Someone who feeds him – and gives him extra treats – is worthy of respect.

- Do not let your Miniature Schnauzer barge through doors ahead of you or leap from the back of the car before you release him. You may need to put your dog on the lead and teach him to "Wait" at doorways and then reward him for letting you go through first.

If your Miniature Schnauzer is progressing well with his retraining programme, think about getting involved with a dog sport, such as agility or heelwork to music. This will give your Miniature Schnauzer a positive outlet for his energies. However, if your Miniature is still trying to take control, or you have any other concerns, do not delay in seeking the help of an animal behaviourist.

**Sometimes a Mini will become possessive about a favourite toy.**

## BARKING

The Miniature is a vocal breed, and, as an alert watch dog, he will warn you when strangers are approaching. However, some Miniatures like the sound of their own voice rather too much, and this can make a dog trying to live with.

A Miniature Schnauzer may bark for the following reasons:

- To warn when strangers are passing
- To get attention
- To demand their own way
- To lay claim to their territory – running along a boundary fence and barking when people pass by.

There is no point in trying to silence your Miniature Schnauzer before he has barked a warning, because this is in his nature – and it also serves a useful purpose. However, he must understand that a warning bark is sufficient, and there is no need to continue barking once the visitors have come into your house, or when strangers have walked past your house.

The best plan is to verbally praise your Miniature Schnauzer for barking a warning, and then reward him with a treat as soon as he is quiet. Do not talk to your dog and do not make eye contact with him until he is quiet, and

**A Miniature Schnauzer is naturally vocal – particularly when he is on watch.**

then instantly reward him. As he begins to get the idea, you can introduce the verbal cue "Quiet". It will not take him long to learn that he must accept your judgment, and he will be rewarded for his initial response, and then again when you tell him it is time to be "Quiet".

Barking to mark a boundary line is more likely to happen if you live in a rural location and passers-by have a novelty value. Try not to let this behaviour become habitual, as it will be far harder to remedy if it has become ingrained. The best

plan is to expose your dogs to a wide variety of different situations, including visiting friends' houses where your dog will not feel territorial and does not feel the need to react.

## INTOLERANCE TO GROOMING

The Miniature Schnauzer is a high-maintenance breed when it comes to coat care, and your dog must learn to accept lengthy periods on the grooming table. If you follow the advice given in this book (See Chapter Five: The Best of Care), you will have accustomed your puppy to grooming and all-over handling at an early age so that he learns to accept the attention. In fact, most Miniature Schnauzer positively enjoy being groomed; they relax completely and enjoy spending quality time with their owners.

However, if a Miniature Schnauzer has not received this early education – or, worse still, he has been badly handled or hurt during a grooming session – he will become highly intolerant. A Miniature Schnauzer has a long memory, and if he has once been ill-treated or experienced pain or discomfort when being groomed, he will not forget. He will become very hard to handle, and, in extreme cases, he may growl or even snap if you attempt to groom him.

Obviously you hope this is a situation that will never arise, but it may be that you have taken on a rescued dog whose grooming needs have been neglected, or your dog may have been roughly handled or ill treated.

If your Miniature Schnauzer resents being groomed, you will need to go right back to basics:

• To begin with, do not put your Miniature Schnauzer on the grooming table, as this will probably have a bad association for him. Select a completely different place – such as the sitting room or even the garden, so you can make a fresh start.

• Attach a lead so you are in control, and, if necessary, recruit a helper, who can hold your dog while you attend to him. Prepare a bowl of tasty treats and have them at the ready.

• To begin with, stroke your Miniature Schnauzer and then reward him with a treat. In this situation, using a clicker can be helpful, as you can click when your dog is quiet and calm, and then reward.

• When your Miniature Schnauzer accepts being stroked all over, be a little more invasive and pick up each paw in turn, look in his ears, and stroke right to the tip of his tail. Remember to reward frequently.

• Now introduce a brush and just lay it on his coat, without attempting to groom him.

Reward him instantly, and then try a couple of brush strokes before rewarding again. If he tries to struggle, be firm, and reward more frequently.

You need to be very patient, and progress in tiny steps, starting with very short grooming sessions where you ask very little of your Miniature Schnauzer; only progress to the next stage when he is totally calm and relaxed. In time, your dog needs to be able to tolerate a complete grooming session, which includes, brushing, combing and clipping, so do not be in a hurry to achieve too much too soon. The aim is to re-educate your Miniature Schnauzer so that he associates grooming with kindness,

consideration – and lots of tasty treats.

### STEALING

Given the chance, a Miniature Schnauzer will try any food once – and that could be anything from flowers to oranges. Food to this breed is like nectar to a bee, and they will steal anything if the opportunity arises.

This is a case where prevention is definitely better than cure, so if you have a Miniature Schnauzer in your house, be on your guard! Never leave food unattended, and make sure rubbish bins – both inside and outside the house – are secure.

Some Miniature Schnauzers will scavenge when they are out on walks, and this can easily lead to

**This is a high-maintenance breed when it comes to coat care, so puppies must get used to grooming and handling from an early age.**

gastric problems. If you are taking your Miniature Schnauzer to an area that is full of 'temptations', it is better to keep him on an extending lead so you have some degree of control.

Remember: if you ask your Miniature Schnauzer to "Leave" something which you consider undesirable, be quick to reward him with a food treat. As far as he is concerned, the 'prize' he found was well worth having – and he should be enticed away with a better reward. In time, he will build up a positive association with the verbal cue "Leave" and come to you, expecting a treat.

## SEPARATION ANXIETY

The Miniature Schnauzer is pretty laid back and will not be easily stressed, particularly if he has a routine, which includes accepting times when he is on his own. When you have built up a relationship with your Miniature Schnauzer, he will have complete trust in you, and he will be perfectly content to wait for you, knowing you always return.

A Miniature Schnauzer should be brought up to accept short periods of separation from his owner, right from the start, so that he sees this as the norm. This is where an indoor crate is invaluable, as you can leave your puppy for short periods, knowing he cannot get up to any mischief. It is a good idea to leave him with a boredom-busting toy so he will be happily occupied in your absence. When you return, do not rush to the crate and make a huge fuss. Wait a few minutes, and then calmly go to the crate and release your dog, telling him how good he has been. If this scenario is repeated a number of times, your Miniature Schnauzer will soon learn that being left on his own is no big deal.

Problems with separation anxiety are most likely to arise if you take on a rescued dog who has major insecurities. You may also find your Miniature Schnauzer hates being left if you have failed to accustom him to short periods of isolation when he was growing up. Separation anxiety is expressed in a number of ways and all are equally distressing for both dog and owner. An anxious dog who is left alone may bark and whine continuously, urinate and defecate, and may be extremely destructive.

There are a number of steps you can take when attempting to solve this problem.

• Put up a baby-gate between adjoining rooms and leave your dog in one room while you are in the other room. Your dog will be able to see you and hear you, but he is learning to cope without being right next to you. Build up the amount of time you can leave your dog in easy stages.

• Buy some boredom-busting toys and fill them with some tasty treats. Whenever you leave your dog, give him a food-filled toy so that he is busy while you are away.

• If you have not used a crate before, it is not too late to start.

**A Miniature Schnauzer's overriding desire is to be with his family.**

Make sure the crate is cosy and train your Miniature Schnauzer to get used to going in his crate while you are in the same room. Gradually build up the amount of time he spends in the crate and then start leaving the room for short periods. When you return, do not make a fuss of your dog. Leave him for five or ten minutes before releasing him, so that he gets used to your comings and goings.

- Pretend to go out, putting on your coat and jangling keys, but do not leave the house. An anxious dog often becomes hyped up by the ritual of leaving and this will help to desensitise him.
- When you go out, leave a radio or a TV on. Some dogs are comforted by hearing voices and background noise when they are left alone.
- Try to make your absences as short as possible when you are first training your dog to accept being on his own.

If you take these steps, your dog should become less anxious and, over a period of time, you should be able to solve the problem. However, if you are failing to make progress, do not delay in calling in expert help.

**You can use a crate so that your Mini Schnauzer can still see you but is learning to spend time on his own.**

## AGGRESSION

Aggression is a complex issue, as there are different causes and the behaviour may be triggered by numerous factors. It may be directed towards people, but, far more commonly it is directed towards other dogs. Aggression in dogs may be the result of:

- Dominance (see page 108).
- Defensive behaviour: This may be induced by fear, pain or punishment.
- Territory: A dog may become aggressive if strange dogs or people enter his territory (which is generally seen as the house and garden).
- Intra-sexual issues: This is aggression between sexes – male-to-male or female-to-female.
- Parental instinct: A mother dog may become aggressive if she is protecting her puppies.

Over the years, the true Miniature Schnauzer has been bred by reputable breeders that have made sound temperament a top priority. Aggression in the Miniature Schnauzer is therefore very rare and would only be present if the dog had been ill treated, inadequately socialised, or found himself in a situation where he had to protect himself.

## NEW CHALLENGES

If you enjoy training your Miniature Schnauzer, you may want to try one of the many dog sports that are now on offer.

## GOOD CITIZEN SCHEME

This is a scheme run by the Kennel Club in the UK and the American Kennel Club in the USA. The schemes promote responsible ownership and help you to train a well-behaved dog who will fit in with the community. The schemes are excellent for all pet owners and they are also a good starting point if you plan to compete with your Miniature Schnauzer when he is older. The KC and the AKC schemes vary in format. In the UK there is a puppy foundation scheme followed by bronze, silver and gold levels with each test becoming progressively more demanding. In the AKC scheme there is a single test.

Some of the exercises include:
- Walking on a loose lead among people and other dogs.
- Recall amid distractions.
- A controlled greeting where dogs stay under control while their owners meet.
- The dog allows all-over grooming and handling by his owner, and also accepts being handled by the examiner.
- Stays, with the owner in sight and then out of sight.
- Food manners, allowing the owner to eat without begging and taking a treat on command.
- Sendaway – sending the dog to his bed.

The tests are designed to show the control you have over your dog and his ability to respond correctly and remain calm in all situations. The Good Citizen Scheme is taught at most training clubs. For more information, log on to the Kennel Club or AKC website (see Appendices).

## COMPETITIVE OBEDIENCE

This is a precision sport that tends to suit breeds such as the Border Collie, the German Shepherd Dog and some of the retriever breeds. However, there is no reason why you should not have a go and see how your Miniature Schnauzer gets on.

There are various levels of achievement, and the exercises get increasingly more demanding as you head up the classes. Marks are lost for even the slightest crooked angle noticed when the dog is sitting and if a dog has a momentary attention deficit or works too far away from his owner

**Teach your Miniature Schnauzer to be a model canine citizen.**

in heelwork, again points will be deducted.

The exercises that must be mastered include the following:
- Heelwork: Dog and handler must complete a set pattern on and off the lead, which includes left turns, right turns, about turns and changes of pace.
- Recall: This may be when the handler is stationary or on the move.
- Retrieve: This may be a dumbbell or any article chosen by the judge.
- Sendaway: The dog is sent to a designated spot and must go into an instant 'Down' until he is recalled by the handler.
- Stays: The dog must stay in the 'Sit' and in the 'Down' for a set amount of time. In advanced classes, the handler is out of sight.
  - Scent: The dog must retrieve a single cloth from a pre-arranged pattern of cloths that has his owner's scent or, in advanced classes, the judge's scent. There may also be decoy cloths.
- Distance control. The dog must execute a series of moves ('Sit', 'Stand', 'Down') without moving from his position and with the handler at a distance.

Even though competitive obedience requires accuracy and precision, make sure you make it fun for your Miniature Schnauzer with lots of praise and rewards so that you motivate him to do his best. Many training clubs run advanced classes for those who want to compete in obedience, or you can hire the services of a professional trainer for one-on-one sessions.

## SHOWING

In your eyes, your Miniature Schnauzer is the most beautiful dog in the world – but would a judge agree? Showing is a highly competitive sport, and, with entry fees and travelling, it can be quite costly. However, many owners get bitten by the showing bug, and their calendar is governed by the dates of the top showing fixtures.

To be successful in the show ring, a Mini must conform as closely as possible to the Breed Standard, which is a written blueprint describing the 'perfect' Miniature Schnauzer (see Chapter Seven). To get started you need to buy a puppy that has show potential and then train him to perform in the ring. A Mini will be 'stacked' so that he stands in the correct show pose. He must gait for the judge in order to show off his natural movement, and he must also be examined by the judge. This involves a detailed hands-on examination, so your Mini must be bombproof when handled by strangers.

Many training clubs hold ringcraft classes, which are run by experienced showgoers. At these classes, you will learn how to handle your Mini in the ring, and you will also find out about rules, procedures and show ring etiquette.

The best plan is to start off at some small, informal shows where

**Showing is highly competitive at the top level.**

you can practise and learn the tricks of the trade before graduating to bigger shows. It's a long haul, starting in the very first puppy class, but the dream is to make your Miniature Schnauzer up into a Champion.

## AGILITY

This fun sport has grown enormously in popularity over the past few years, and the fast-moving Miniature Schnauzer is more than capable of competing to a high level. If you fancy having a go, make sure you have good control over your Miniature and keep him slim. Agility is a very physical sport, which demands fitness from both dog and handler.

In agility competitions, each dog must complete a set course over a series of obstacles, which include:

- Jumps (upright hurdles and long jump, varying in height – small, medium and large, depending on the size of the dog)
- Weaves
- A-frame
- Dog walk
- Seesaw
- Tunnels (collapsible and rigid)
- Tyre

Dogs may compete in Jumping classes, with jumps, tunnels and weaves, or in Agility classes, which have the full set of equipment. Faults are awarded for poles down on the jumps, missed contact points on the A-frame, dog walk and seesaw, and refusals. If a dog takes the wrong course, he is eliminated. The winner is the dog that completes the course in the fastest time with no faults. As you progress up the

## COMPETING IN AGILITY

The quick-thinking agile Miniature Schnauzer excels at this sport.

**Clearing the hurdles…**

**Powering out of the tunnel…**

**Negotiating the dog walk…**

**At the top of the A frame.**

levels, courses become progressively harder with more twists, turns and changes of direction.

If you want to get involved in agility, you will need to find a club that specialises in the sport (see Appendices). You will not be allowed to start training until your Miniature Schnauzer is 12 months old and you cannot compete until he is 18 months old. This rule is for the protection of the dog, who may suffer injury if he puts strain on bones and joints while he is still growing.

### FLYBALL

The Miniature Schnauzer is not a natural retriever, but with training he can enjoy the hurly burly and excitement of competing in flyball.

Flyball is a team sport; the dogs love it and it is undoubtedly the noisiest of all the canine sports!

Four dogs are selected to run in a relay race against an opposing team. The dogs are sent out by their handlers to jump four hurdles, catch the ball from the flyball box, and then return over the hurdles. At the top level, this sport is fast and furious, and although it is dominated by Border Collies, the Miniature Schnauzer can make a contribution. This is particularly true in multibreed competitions, where the team is made up of four dogs of different breeds and only one can be a Border Collie or a Working Sheepdog. Points are awarded to dogs and teams. Annual awards are given to top dogs and top teams, and

**Keep your half of the bargain and you will be rewarded with a companion that is second to none.**

milestone awards are given out to dogs as they attain points throughout their flyballing careers.

### DANCING WITH DOGS

This sport is relatively new, but it is becoming increasingly popular. It is very entertaining to watch, but it is certainly not as simple as it looks. To perform a choreographed routine to music with your Miniature Schnauzer demands a huge amount of training. However, this is a discipline that suits the Miniature as he can do moves, such as standing on his hindlegs, with ease, and he loves the opportunity to show off.

Dancing with dogs is divided into two categories: heelwork to music and canine freestyle. In heelwork to music, the dog must

work closely with his handler and show a variety of close 'heelwork' positions. In canine freestyle, the routine can be more flamboyant, with the dog working at a distance from the handler and performing spectacular tricks. Routines are judged on style and presentation, content and accuracy.

### SUMMING UP

The Miniature Schnauzer is a truly outstanding companion dog – and once you have owned one, no other breed will do. He is intelligent, fun-loving, and loyal. Make sure you keep your half of the bargain: spend time socialising and training your Miniature Schnauzer so that you can be proud to take him anywhere and he will always be a credit to you.

# THE PERFECT MINIATURE SCHNAUZER

## Chapter 7

The majority of those buying a Miniature Schnauzer will have done so because of the breed's character and splendid qualities as a family companion. The non-shedding coat, the choice of attractive colours, and their hardy size and sturdiness all contribute to the breed's growing popularity.

For most people, reading the Breed Standard will not have been high on their list of priorities before or after getting a puppy. In some ways, this is a pity because the ideals, essential requirements and faults covered in it encapsulate so much of what is considered important and desirable, as well as what is wrong and undesirable. The Breed Standard gives a word picture of what the breed should be, based on its purpose and looks, which need to be fully understood if a breed is to develop and progress along the lines originally intended, without change or exaggeration.

Breed Standards are not only a guide for judges and sincere breeders, but also for those breeding the occasional litter, as the aim should always be one of improvement.

In Britain, although breed clubs are consulted over changes or any new proposals, Breed Standards are the property of the Kennel Club. In other parts of the world they are the interest of individual breed clubs, giving more direct control to those seriously interested and involved, rather than to a controlling administrative authority. With today's liberal thinking, such bodies seek uniformity covering all breeds, rather than being specific to each breed.

The first Breed Standard was drawn up in 1880 in Bavaria, southern Germany of today, the area of the breed's original recognition and development. Although there have been changes, these have not altered the essence for what the breed's founding fathers intended. They were striving for a sturdy, reliable, robust, sound, handy-sized, adaptable, intelligent working breed, not a terrier or a toy dog. These qualities and aims have been translated into the splendid breed and family companion we have today.

## GOVERNING BODIES

The current Kennel Club (KC) Breed Standard was updated in November 2010, with inclusion of the colour white (see page 127). This followed a previous

**Ch. Malenda Master Blend at Risepark: An outstanding show dog in the UK**
*Photo: Sally Anne Thompson.*

**Am. Ch. Dorem Display: This dog had a phenomenal influence on American Miniature Schnauzers.**

amendment in 2009, when the Kennel Club added the Fit For Purpose clause which prefaces all Breed Standards. This states:
*"A Breed Standard is the guideline which describes the ideal characteristics, temperament and appearance of a breed, but it also ensures that the breed is fit for function. Absolute soundness is essential. Breeders and judges should at all times be careful to avoid obvious conditions or exaggerations which would be detrimental in any way to the health, welfare or soundness of this breed. From time to time certain conditions or exaggerations may be considered to have the potential to affect dogs in some breeds adversely; judges and breeders are requested to refer to the Kennel Club website for details of any such current issues. If a feature or quality is desirable, it should only be present in the right measure."*

This clause is intended to discourage exaggeration in some breeds, which is fine. However, it will not stop there, especially when taken into consideration with the Faults clause we now have. This generalised form of judging is becoming the norm, and attitudes towards a breed's special features, movement and faults are becoming less understood and appreciated. In Miniatures we are finding the more elegant Terrier look and body winning over the correct sturdy and well-ribbed dog, and the eye-catching, extended side-gaiting is being preferred to that which is correctly seen in the straight up and down.

The American Kennel Club (AKC) places the Miniature Schnauzer in the Terrier Group, whereas it is classed as a Utility breed in the UK. The AKC Breed

Standard was last revised in 1991. At the present time, the colour white – now accepted by the Kennel Club in the UK – is not recognised.

The Federation Cynologique Internationale (FCI), which is the governing body for Europe, South America, South Africa and most of the Asian countries, has a sub-section for Schnauzers and Pinschers; it was the first authority to accept white as a recognised colour for Miniature Schnauzers. The FCI adopts the Standard from a breed's country of origin.

With British Miniature Schnauzers carrying so much American breeding, along with the relaxing of the quarantine regulations, giving freer access to our neighbours in Europe and Scandinavia, as well as making importing easier, it is interesting to see how the American,

# WHAT IS TYPE?

It is the judge's job to find the Miniature Schnauzer that most closely adheres to the Breed Standard.

Before considering the Breed Standard in detail, we need to understand the meaning of type. This is the shape, balance and outline that gives each breed its 'look,' which could not be mistaken for any breed other than the one it is. It is important to breed and judge principally for type, along with the essentials asked for in the Breed Standard, otherwise a breed will become untypical, with little uniformity, and without a readily recognisable 'look'. A dog must be correct for breed type to be worthy of its breed name.

Federation Cynologique Internationale (FCI) and the Kennel Club Breed Standards differ.

The Kennel Club has remained closest to the original. The FCI, coming as it does from Germany, the breed motherland, has become much more detailed, listing far more faults, along with a wide range of disqualifications. As a result it is perhaps easier to accept the safety of average, rather than the outstanding, despite any faults. The dog that is outstanding in whatever way will often look different from the rest, so the qualities are overlooked rather than appreciated. An absence of faults does not necessarily mean quality. Quality is indefinable: something that looks right and draws attention, and is the hallmark of an outstanding dog.

## ANALYSIS OF THE BREED STANDARDS

### GENERAL APPEARANCE AND CHARACTERISTICS
*KC*
Sturdily built, robust, sinewy, nearly square (length of body equal to height at shoulders). Expression keen and attitude alert. Correct conformation is of more importance than colour or other 'beauty' points.

Well balanced, smart, stylish and adaptable.

*AKC*
The Miniature Schnauzer is a robust, active dog of terrier type, resembling his larger cousin, the Standard Schnauzer, in general appearance, and of an alert, active disposition. *Faults*: Type – Toyishness, ranginess or coarseness.

*FCI*
Small, strong, stocky rather than slim, rough coated, elegant. A reduced image of the Schnauzer without the

**The Miniature Schnauzer is well balanced, smart and stylish.**
*Photo: Sally Anne Thompson.*

drawback of a dwarfed appearance.

**IMPORTANT PROPORTIONS**
**Square build in which the height at the withers is nearly equal to the body length.**
**The length of the head (measured from the tip of the nose to the occiput) corresponds to half the length of the topline (measured from the withers to the set on of the tail).**

This opening paragraph gives the overall 'look' for the breed, asking for a sturdy body but not overdone or over muscled. "Nearly square", referred to in the KC Standard, is a clearly defined measurement from breastbone to buttocks and withers (shoulders) to ground. This ensures the construction of a breed that is capable of moving over distances for a period of time, without tiring. The importance of expression and attitude is emphasised, both important in giving Miniature Schnauzers their individuality and appeal.

The reference in the KC Standard to construction being of more importance than colour or other 'beauty' points was added in 1954 when the breed was being re-established in Britain after the war years. At the time, the more robust, sturdy American type versus a more 'toyish' Continental look and colouring were matters of disagreement within the breed. It is important to understand there was never any intention to downgrade the importance of the colours, particularly the unique pepper and salt. This opening paragraph also reminds us that the breed was highly regarded for its qualities of character and sturdiness and is not a 'beauty' breed.

In America, shortly after being given separate status, the Miniature Schnauzer has been classified in the Terrier Group, hence the reference to 'being of terrier type' in the AKC Standard.

Short and to the point, the characteristics – "Well balanced, smart, stylish and adaptable" – sum up the Miniature Schnauzer so well. Be it as a family companion, a show dog, or a competitor in any other dog related activity, the Miniature Schnauzer loves to be involved.

"Well balanced" means unexaggerated and all the parts in harmony with one another. Miniature Schnauzers are certainly "smart and stylish", which shows in the way a dog carries himself, along with his innate sense of importance. The breed's adaptability is one of the most valued characteristics; a Miniature Schnauzer is content to settle into whatever situation he finds himself.

## AN IMPECCABLE TEMPERAMENT

These contrasting photos epitomise the Miniature Schnauzer's temperament.

An alert watch dog who is always ready to investigate.

The gentle family companion who tunes into the feelings of his family.

## TEMPERAMENT

### KC

Alert, reliable and intelligent. Primarily a companion dog.

### AKC

The typical Miniature Schnauzer is alert and spirited, yet obedient to command. He is friendly, intelligent and willing to please. He should never be overaggressive or timid.

### FCI

His nature is similar to that of the Schnauzer and is determined by the temperament and the behaviour of a small dog. Intelligence, fearlessness, endurance and alertness make the Miniature Schnauzer an agreeable house dog as well as a watch and companion dog which can be kept even in a small apartment without problems.

The temperament is quite exceptional and matchless. Although trimmed out like a terrier, they are not so in temperament or behaviour, nor are they aggressive or jealous. The breed is ideal as a housedog, always being aware of what is going on, and vocal rather than aggressive. The breed's splendid temperament and adaptability has been greatly valued by breeders over the years, and are always important considerations with all matings. The breed has an excellent and growing reputation as an ideal family dog – loving, sensible, reliable, and adaptable, all with an endearing nature.

## HEAD AND SKULL

### KC

Head strong and of good length, narrowing from ears to eyes and then gradually forward toward end of nose. Upper part of the head (occiput to the base of forehead) moderately broad between ears. Flat, creaseless forehead; well-muscled but not too strongly developed cheeks. Medium stop to accentuate prominent eyebrows. Powerful

Viewed from the front, the muzzle ends in a blunt wedge.

muzzle ending in a moderately blunt line, with bristly, stubby moustache and chin whiskers. Ridge of nose straight and running almost parallel to extension of forehead. Nose black with wide nostrils. Lips tight but not overlapping.

## AKC

Strong and rectangular, its width diminishing slightly from ears to eyes, and again to the tip of the nose. The forehead is unwrinkled. The *topskull* is flat and fairly long. The foreface is parallel to the topskull, with a slight stop, and it is at least as long as the topskull. The *muzzle* is strong in proportion to the skull; it ends in a moderately blunt manner, with thick whiskers which accentuate the rectangular shape of the head.
*Faults*: Head coarse and cheeky.

## FCI
### CRANIAL REGION
Skull: Strong, long without markedly protruding occiput. The head should be in keeping with the dog's force. The forehead is flat, without wrinkles and parallel to the bridge of nose.
Stop: Appears well defined due to the brows

### FACIAL REGION
Nose: Well developed nose leather, always black.
Muzzle: Ending in a blunt wedge. Bridge of nose straight.
Lips: Black, smooth and tight-fitting to the jaws. Corners of lips closed.

There is a lot of detail given as to what makes a good head, which is always an important and distinguishing feature with any breed. Although emphasis is on strength, the importance of the back skull, foreface and muzzle being in proportion and in balance with each other is stressed as well as having clean cheeks. The head should be in no way coarse; it should balance and compliment the sturdy body – another essential requirement. The proportions of the skull and foreface are likened to those of the common house brick, where the width is half the length. This reminds us that the Miniature head is not narrow or short, and the length of the skull and the foreface should be the same.

A flat, unwrinkled forehead is

**When looking at the head in profile, there should be a medium stop (the step up between the skull and the nasal bone) to accentuate the prominent eyebrows.**

*Photo: Sally Ann Thompson.*

straightforward; the flatness is important and should always be felt for, as rounded or domed skulls are not unknown and can be disguised by good trimming. There should always be a good solid feel and look to the muzzle, especially in front of the eyes, otherwise the muzzle is said to fall away, which is a serious fault. This can be disguised with trimming, so should always be felt for.

A longer foreface is more acceptable; a short one less desirable and is often seen with an ultra-short body. It should also be remembered that an overlong foreface can give rise to a head that is terrier-like in looks and proportions. A strong, broad muzzle enables the teeth to be of good size (once required in the Standard) with the correct

placement. It also gives a good strong under jaw.

Asking for a nose that is black ensures tough skin and good pigment; wide nostrils compliment the good heart and lung room called for. Lips must be tight but not overlapping, and this, along with the stubbly moustache, are reminders of the breed's use as a catcher of vermin – the muzzle and lips are designed to prevent vermin from hanging on and to protect the dog from bites.

Looking at the AKC Standard, there is a marked difference in head properties with demands for it to be narrower and longer, particularly the foreface. There is also a less pronounced stop (the indentation between the eyebrows) and a deep-set smaller eye, giving much more the look

and expression of a terrier. Nowadays, the breed is much more vulnerable to becoming a terrier in America than ever in the past.

Although the breed has been in the Terrier Group for many years, breeders and judges have always understood, bred and judged to those important differences that make the Miniature Schnauzer the breed it is, rather than a terrier. Today, this is not so often the case, with the growing movement towards a more generalised approach to judging and breed requirements, not only in America but also in Britain and elsewhere. Understanding and upholding these essentials will lessen, and yet they are at the very heart of knowing and understanding a breed, and of good judging.

The ears are V-shaped and set on high. When they are not cropped they fold close to the skull.
*Photo: Sally Anne Thompson.*

Cropped ears have a significant effect on the Miniature Schnauzer's expression.
*Photo: Jauksen.*

## EARS

### KC

Neat V-shaped, set high and dropping forward to temple.

### AKC

When cropped, the ears are identical in shape and length, with pointed tips. They are in balance with the head and not exaggerated in length. They are set high on the skull and carried perpendicularly at the inner edges, with as little bell as possible along the outer edges. When uncropped, the ears are small and V-shaped, folding close to the skull.

### FCI

Drop ears, set high, V-shaped with inner edges lying close to the cheeks, evenly carried, turned forward towards temples. Folds parallel, should not be above the top of the skull.

The ears play an important part in giving the right look to the expression and head properties; their thickness, size and shape having much to do with this. The AKC still allows cropped ears, which, again, has a major effect on the facial expression.

"Neat" means they balance and are in keeping with the head.

"V-shaped" indicates that round or heavy, hound-like ears are undesirable.

"Set high" simply means the ears fold above the level of the back skull, but not high as in Fox Terriers.

"Dropping forward to temple" indicates where the tip of the ear should fall and, importantly, also conveys that the ear is set to the side of the head, and not set on top, to fall to the eyebrows, as do those of Fox Terriers with their narrow heads. The ears falling as they should enables the Miniature head to have strength and be in balance with the sturdy body.

The eyes are dark, oval in shape, with a keen expression.

## EYES

### KC

**Medium-sized, dark oval, set forward with arched, bushy eyebrows.**

### AKC

**Small, dark brown and deep-set. They are oval in appearance and keen in expression.**
*Faults:* **Eyes light and/or large and prominent in appearance.**

### FCI

**Medium sized, oval, facing forward, dark with lively expression. Eyelids close fitting.**

A straightforward description that makes a small, round, full or oriental-looking eye, as well as those light-coloured or excessively dark, completely wrong. "Set forward" means they are not deeply or opaquely set, which would give an untypical expression.

Colour, placement and shape of the eyes, the size and shape of the ears, the ear carriage, together with the general shape of the head and the dark mask (the dark hairs on top of the foreface), which is no longer asked for as part of the Breed Standard, all combine to give the breed the distinctive 'down the nose' look and expression.

## MOUTH

### KC

**Jaws strong, with perfect regular and complete scissor bite, i.e. the upper teeth closely overlapping the lower teeth, and set square to the jaw.**

### AKC

**The teeth meet in a scissors bite. That is, the upper front teeth overlap the lower front teeth in such a manner that the inner surface of the upper incisors barely touches the**

outer surface of the lower
incisors when the mouth is
closed.

*Faults*: Bite – Undershot or
overshot jaw. Level bite.

*FCI*
Strong upper and lower jaw. The
complete scissor bite (42 pure
white teeth according to the
dentition formula) is strongly
developed and firmly closing.
The chewing muscles are
strongly developed but the
cheeks must not interfere with
the rectangular shape of the
head (with the beard).

The scissor bite, as described, is
the only correct one for the breed.
Overshot is when the upper jaw
overlaps the bottom, which so
often goes with a weak, narrow
underjaw. Undershot is when the
lower jaw protrudes beyond the
upper. A level bite is where the

top and bottom line of teeth meet
edge to edge and are level with
each other, causing the biting
edges to wear down.

Faults with teeth or jaw
alignment should always be taken
seriously and are one of the most
difficult to eradicate.

The FCI calls for a full
complement of 42 teeth, whereas
the British and American
Standards are only concerned for
the bite to be correct.

## NECK
*KC*
Moderately long, strong and
slightly arched. Skin close to the
throat. Neck set cleanly on
shoulders.

*AKC*
Strong and well arched,
blending into the shoulders,
and with the skin fitting tightly
at the throat.

*FCI*
The strong, muscular neck is
nobly arched, blending
smoothly into the withers.
Strongly set on, slim, nobly
curved, corresponding to the
dog's force. Throat skin tight-
fitting without folds.

A moderately long neck
compliments the not overdone
sturdy body and balanced head
properties. The neck, being strong
and slightly arched, gives a touch
of elegance and flexibility to the
head, enabling it to be carried
proudly and high, which is very
much a breed characteristic. The
skin should lie close to the throat,
precluding any throatiness,
something that is usually seen
with a short neck.

"Set clean on shoulders" means
the neck and shoulders are
completely interdependent with
each other and should flow and
blend into each other, as well as
smoothly into the backline.

## FOREQUARTERS
*KC*
Shoulders flat and well laid.
Forelegs straight when viewed
from any angle. Muscles smooth
and lithe rather than
prominent. Bone strong,
straight and carried well down
to feet. Elbows close to the body
and pointing directly forwards.

*AKC*
Forelegs are straight and
parallel when viewed from all
sides. They have strong pasterns
and good bone. They are
separated by a fairly deep

The neck is moderately long and set cleanly on the shoulders.

brisket which precludes a pinched front. The elbows are close, and the ribs spread gradually from the first rib so as to allow space for the elbows to move close to the body. *Fault:* Loose elbows.

The sloping *shoulders* are muscled, yet flat and clean. They are well laid back, so that from the side the tips of the shoulder blades are in a nearly vertical line above the elbow. The tips of the blades are placed closely together. They slope forward and downward at an angulation which permits the maximum forward extension of the forelegs without binding or effort. Both the shoulder blades and upper arms are long, permitting depth of chest at the brisket.

*FCI*
Seen from the front, the front legs are strong, straight and not close together. Seen from the side, the forearms are straight. Shoulders: The shoulder blade lies close against the rib cage and is well muscled on both sides of the shoulder bone, protruding over the points of the thoracic vertebrae. As sloping as possible and well laid back, forming an angle of approximately 50 degrees to the horizontal.
Upper arm: Lying close to the body, strong and well muscled, forming an angle of 95° to 105° to the shoulder blade.
Elbows: Close fitting, turning neither in nor out.
Forearm: Viewed from all sides,

completely straight, strongly developed and well muscled. Carpal joint: Strong, firm, barely standing out against the structure of the forearm. Pastern: Seen from the front, vertical. Seen from the side slightly sloping towards the ground, strong and slightly springy.

The forequarters give the reach (stride) for good ground coverage; the hindquarters provide the power. It is in the front assembly we find the reason for the difference between the straight, more terrier front that gives a restricted stilted movement, instead of an effortless, more flowing stride correct for the Miniature Schnauzer.

Differences in front movement mainly comes about through the position and length of the shoulder blade (scapula) and upperarm (humerus). Before looking at these, we need to appreciate that bones in the forequarters are attached to the skeleton by muscles and tendons, giving the front assembly its flexibility. The muscles should be smooth and the shoulders should lie flat, to create a lithe and supple body, with good tone, which is all helped by sensible exercise. An overdeveloped body and muscling can only be a disadvantage to the individual's general wellbeing and detract from the typical easy tireless movement.

The correctly constructed forequarters find the shoulder blade and upper arm almost equal

in length at about a 100-degree angle to each other. The shoulder blade should lie well back and flat against the rib cage. The upper arm should meet the top of the leg at the elbow, to give a good forechest, but also enabling the front legs to stand under the dog, so distributing the body weight evenly. Ideally, the shoulder

**The forelegs are straight and the elbows are tucked close to the body.**

**The back is strong and is slightly higher at the shoulder than at the quarters.**

blades should be about an inch (2.5 cm) apart at the withers (top of the shoulder), which can be easily felt for. The shoulder bones and their angles need to be correct and in alignment, as this area absorbs much of the natural jarring occurring with movement.

When the angle is more than ideal, it makes the upper arm straighter and places it well ahead of the rib cage, giving little forechest and an undesirable, straight front with a short stepping movement. The front legs are also placed more forward, rather than correctly under the body.

When the upper arm is correct but the angle greater, it places the shoulder blades higher in the neck than desired, giving an illusion of a short neck.

When the shoulder blades are well placed but have a greater angle, it gives heavy shoulders and a 'fleshy' pigeon chest, again

incorrect for the breed. It also makes the dog short on the leg and dumpy looking, as the height at the croup (root of tail) is higher than at the shoulders.

Good, strong, straight bone, carried well down, ensures it is adequate to support a sturdy body and straight legs.

Elbows should lie close to the body and point forward, to ensure straight and controlled front movement – with no evidence of undesirable looseness. The pasterns (wrist on the front legs) are not described. They need to be slightly bent and flexible, allowing for easy movement, especially over rough ground, and movement shock is again readily dispersed.

## BODY
### KC
**Chest moderately broad, with deep visible strong breastbone reaching at least to height of**

elbow rising slightly backward to loins.

Back strong and straight, slightly higher at shoulder than at hindquarters, with short, well developed loins. Ribs well sprung. Length of body equal to height from top of withers to ground.

### AKC
Short and deep, with the brisket extending at least to the elbows. Ribs are well sprung and deep, extending well back to a short loin. The underbody does not present a tucked up appearance at the flank. The *backline* is straight; it declines slightly from the withers to the base of the tail. The withers form the highest point of the body. The overall length from chest to buttocks appears to equal the height at the withers.
*Faults*: Chest too broad or shallow in brisket. Hollow or roach back.

### FCI
**Topline: Slightly sloping from withers towards rear.**
**Withers: Forming the highest point in topline.**
**Back: Strong, short and taut.**
**Loins: Short, strong and deep. The distance from the last rib to the hip is short to make the dog appear compact.**
**Croup: Slightly rounded and imperceptibly blending into tail set on.**
**Chest: Moderately broad, oval in diameter, reaching to the elbows. The forechest is distinctly marked by the point**

of the sternum.

**Underline and belly: Flanks not too tucked up, forming a well curved line with the underside of the ribcage.**

This paragraph gets to the very heart of the breed's 'look' and sturdiness. Everything else asked for in the Standard compliments what is called for here – but in moderation – so ensuring the breed is not coarse or exaggerated

It is well and precisely worded to give no doubt about the importance of a deep, roomy, well-ribbed body, with a noticeably strong breastbone. The significance of the breastbone reaching to at least the height of the elbow (the minimum requirement) is for the body to be carried *between* the legs and not on top. This provides a lower and better centre of gravity for a working dog, where ease of effort and endurance are more important than for a breed requiring speed.

"Rising slightly backwards towards the loins" emphasises there should be good depth and length with the ribcage, with ribs extended well back. This makes a narrow flat-sided ribcage with noticeable tuck-up at the loin, and a body carried on the legs rather than coming down between them – all completely wrong.

Equally wrong are the overdone well-rounded barrel ribs, which prevent the front legs fitting close to the body as they should, and makes them bowed.

Ideally the correct ribs are long

and elliptical and angle back from the spinal column, with the first five being flatter to allow for the free movement of the forelegs.

The requirements for the back (topline) are sometimes misunderstood. The topline from the shoulder blades (withers) to the tail should be straight and firm, sloping slightly without sagging or dipping or rising over the loin. This is clearly seen in profile movement, but is minimised with good grooming.

The breed has a well-developed and long rib cage with a prominent breastbone, but it is important to understand that the correct shortness of the back comes from the short, well-developed loins and not a short body. Failure to appreciate this difference can also come about by

**The hindquarters are well muscled, providing the power and strength for movement.**

accepting what is seen with the eyes, rather than what is found by the hands. The robust, well-ribbed dog will always give the impression of being longer and bigger.

Asking for the loins to be well developed helps prevent any problems or weaknesses developing through a weak spine.

## HINDQUARTERS
### KC
**Thighs slanting and flat but strongly muscled. Hindlegs (upper lower thighs) at first vertical to the stifle; from stifle to hock in line with the extension of the upper neckline from hock vertical to ground.**

### AKC
**The hindquarters have strong-muscled, slanting thighs. They are well bent at the stifles. There is sufficient angulation so that, in stance, the hocks extend beyond the tail. The hindquarters never appear overbuilt or higher than the shoulders. The rear pasterns are short and, in stance, perpendicular to the ground and, when viewed from the rear, are parallel to each other.**
*Faults*: **Sickle hocks, cow hocks, open hocks or bowed hindquarters.**

### FCI
**Standing obliquely when seen from the side, standing parallel but not close together when seen from the rear.**
**Upper thigh: Moderately long, broad and strongly muscled.**

**Stifle: Turning neither in nor out.**
**Lower thigh: Long, strong and sinewy, running into a strong hock.**
**Hock: Very well angulated, strong, firm, turning neither in nor out.**
**Metatarsus: Short, vertical to the ground.**

The hindquarters provide the power and strength for movement. Because the Miniature Schnauzer is not a one-pace breed, he should be well muscled but not overdone (as we see with running breeds, such as the Greyhound or Whippet).

The rest of the paragraph refers to an imaginary line drawn from the knee, or lower part of the hindlegs, through the neckline at the top of the withers. When correct this will show that the individual is evenly balanced, with the correct angles of the bones in the shoulders and hindquarters complimenting each other. Hocks should be vertical to the ground in a natural stance that puts the hind legs correctly underneath. This will also mean that, in movement, the centre of gravity will be correct, allowing the effort of movement to be both powerful and effective, and also evenly absorbed throughout the body, causing no wear and tear on the joints.

Although not mentioned, a neat hock is considered important and desirable since this enhances balance, as well as firmness with movement. A long hock gives a restricted, more stilted movement, covering little ground and lacking both power and drive. It can also have an unwanted effect on the topline, making it rise over the loin. Two other common faults found with weak, long hocks, are cow hocks when they turning inwards, and open hocks when they turn out.

There are three main bones in the hindquarters; through their angles to each other and

**The feet are round and cat-like with dark nails and black pads.**

individual lengths, these control how the hindquarters are shaped to be either correct, straight, or over-angulated. Straight hindquarters are more usually poorly muscled and narrow, pushing what power there is upwards rather than forward.

Over-angulated hindquarters tend to be weak, having bones that are longer than ideal. Again, the power is upwards and not correctly forward. Correct hindquarters with the right-length bones and angles – and with good muscling – gives strong, powerful movement.

Also required, but not mentioned, is the need for good buttocks extending beyond the tail. This balances with the good forechest and ensures the hindquarters are well fleshed, muscled and powerful.

## FEET
### KC
**Short, round, cat-like, compact with close, arched toes, dark nails, and black pads. Feet pointing forward.**

### AKC
**Short and round (cat feet) with thick, black pads. The toes are arched and compact.**

### FCI
**Short and round. Toes well-knit and arched (cat foot) with short dark nails and resistant pads.**

It will take some time before the undocked tail (left) reaches a level of consistency within the breed. In the US, the tail can still be docked (right).

This precise paragraph asks for the feet to be neat and compact, not spread out. Black pads are tough-skinned and dark nails indicate good pigmentation. Forward-pointing feet reminds of the importance for strong but flexible pasterns and straight movement, which are needed to cope with varying conditions underfoot.

## TAIL
### KC
**Previously customarily docked.**
**Docked: Set on and carried high, customarily docked to three joints.**
**Undocked: Set on and carried high, of moderate length to give general balance to the dog. Thick at root and tapering towards the top, as straight as possible, carried jauntily.**

### AKC
**Set high and carried erect. It is docked only long enough to be clearly visible over the backline of the body when the dog is in proper length of coat.**
***Fault*: Tail set too low.**

### FCI
**Natural; a sabre or sickle carriage is sought after.**

The AKC still allows the tail to be docked, which gives a smart, clean outline. In countries governed by the KC and FCI Standards, the tail is undocked. This leaves us having to decide whether to make a serious effort for a correct tail, or accept what comes. The latter option will lead to considerable diversity with what it seen, which could well become accepted over a period of time. The big temptation will be to continue to accept those that curl or flop over the hip as these, when seen in profile, are nearest to the docked look but are now completely wrong.

The tail required is erect and in balance with the rest of the dog, particularly in length and thickness. Ideally, it should not be above the line of the head carriage. Again, it is stressed the the tail is in balance with the whole dog.

"Set on and carried high" asks for the croup not to noticeably curve, as in the continental Standards, but to be flat and so enable the tail to be better carried erect. It should not lie over the back.

"Carried jauntily" describes the correct tail carriage well and reflects the breed's nature.

A noticeable difference in the FCI Standard is with the croup, which is rounded rather than flat, as with the Kennel Club and American Standards. The rounded croup gives a lower tail set and a natural tail that curls or lies over the back, rather than being erect, as the flat croup will give.

## GAIT/MOVEMENT
### KC
Free, balanced and vigorous with good reach in forequarters and good driving power in hindquarters. Topline remains level in action.

### AKC
The trot is the gait at which movement is judged. When approaching, the forelegs, with elbows close to the body, move straight forward, neither too close nor too far apart. Going away, the hind legs are straight and travel in the same planes as the forelegs.
*Note: It is generally accepted that when a full trot is achieved, the rear legs continue to move in the same planes as the forelegs, but a very slight inward inclination will occur. It begins at the point of the shoulder in front and at the hip joint in the rear. Viewed from the front or rear, the legs are straight from these points to the pads. The degree of inward inclination is almost imperceptible in a Miniature Schnauzer that has correct movement. It does not justify moving close, toeing in, crossing, or moving out at the elbows.*

Viewed from the side, the forelegs have good reach, while the hind legs have strong drive, with good pickup of hocks. The feet turn neither inward nor outward.
*Faults*: Single tracking, sidegaiting, paddling in front, or hackney action. Weak rear action.

### FCI
Flexible, elegant, agile, free and ground covering. The forelegs swinging as far forward as possible, the hind legs, ground covering and springy, provide the necessary drive. The front leg of one side and the hind leg of the other side move forward at the same time. The back, the ligaments and the joints are firm.

Although breed type is the most important consideration, soundness is not far behind.

A smooth, effortless yet powerful gait, covering plenty of ground and moving with purpose, is what is wanted. With good movement, when coming forward or moving away, the front and hindlegs and feet are straight and parallel and should not be too far apart or too close together. With the correct powerful 'push off' with the hocks, the soles of the rear pads are clearly seen.

In profile, the reach with the front legs and ground coverage are evident. With the hindlegs, the hocks come under the body before pushing off with a powerful, driving movement. Stiff or stilted movement, as well as any lack of rear power and drive, are untypical. Profile movement also shows the overall look and style, as well as if the topline sags or dips, or if the rump is high.

## COAT
### KC
Harsh, wiry and short enough for smartness, dense undercoat. Clean on neck and shoulders,

**Movement should be smooth and effortless but a dog should move with purpose.**
*Photo: www.dog-photography.co.uk*

The bushy eyebrows and full beard are typical Schnauzer characteristics.

ears and skull. Harsh hair on legs. Furnishings fairly thick not silky.

## AKC

Double, with hard, wiry, outer coat and close undercoat. The head, neck, ears, chest, tail, and body coat must be plucked. When in show condition, the body coat should be of sufficient length to determine texture. Close covering on neck, ears and skull. Furnishings are fairly thick but not silky. *Faults*: Coat too soft or too smooth and slick in appearance.

## FCI

The coat should be wiry, harsh and dense. It consists of a dense undercoat and a not too short top coat, lying close to the body. The top coat is rough and sufficiently long to allow the checking of its texture; it is neither bristly nor wavy. The hair on the limbs tends to be less harsh. Coat short on forehead and ears. Typical characteristics are the not too soft beard on the muzzle and the bushy eyebrows which slightly shade the eyes. Skin: Tight fitting over the whole body.

Because of the breed's working background, and uniqueness with the colours, coat has always been important. The harsh, wiry, outer coat protects against the elements; the dense, softer undercoat insulates. The coat requirements have not really changed since first being drawn up, although grooming and presentation certainly has – not necessarily for the better. Nowadays, the breed is ultra smart whereas there should be a more rugged look to their appearance. Interestingly, in the years when points were given, the highest were allocated for coat.

Bearing in mind that early Schnauzers were serious working dogs, which would have been shaggy and somewhat unkempt, it makes me wonder if references to shortness with the coat were to smarten the breed and make it look special and more presentable. Up to then, their reputation and appeal had always been for character, intelligence and ability rather than looks.

Good, harsh coat texture always needs to be hand stripped to be at its best. Clippering will only soften and spoil the colour. The undercoat also needs to be controlled, otherwise it will cause the topcoat to lift and become shapeless, so taking away the breed's smartness and sharp outline. Although harsh furnishings are called for – and at one time were more essential than they are today – they will never be as harsh as the body coat, simply because of the attention given to everyday cleanliness and grooming that goes with being a housedog and having the furnishings washed. It can be readily appreciated that soft or silky furnishings are incorrect for the breed.

## COLOUR
### KC
All pepper and salt colours in even proportions, or pure black, or white or black and silver. That is solid black with silver markings on eyebrow, muzzle, chest and brisket, and on the forelegs below the point of elbow, on inside of hindlegs below the stifle joint (knee), on vent and under tail.

### AKC
The recognized colors are

**The striking combination of black and silver is seen far less than pepper and salt.**

pepper and salt, black and silver and solid black. All colors have uniform skin pigmentation, i.e. no white or pink skin patches shall appear anywhere on the dog.

*Pepper and salt* – The typical pepper and salt color of the topcoat results from the combination of black and white banded hairs and solid black and white unbanded hairs, with the banded hairs predominating. Acceptable are all shades of pepper and salt, from light to dark mixtures with tan shadings permissible in the banded or unbanded hair of the topcoat. In pepper and salt dogs, the pepper and salt mixture fades out to light gray or silver white in the eyebrows,

whiskers, cheeks, under throat, inside ears, across chest, under tail, leg furnishings, and inside hind legs. It may or may not also fade out on the underbody. However, if so, the lighter underbody hair is not to rise higher on the sides of the body than the front elbows.

*Black and Silver* – The black and silver generally follows the same pattern as the pepper and salt. The entire pepper and salt section must be black. The black color in the topcoat of the black and silver is a true rich color with black undercoat. The stripped portion is free from any fading or brown tinge and the underbody should be dark.

*Black* – Black is the only solid color allowed. Ideally, the black color in the topcoat is a true rich glossy solid color with the undercoat being less intense, a soft matting shade of black. This is natural and should not be penalized in any way. The stripped portion is free from any fading or brown tinge. The scissored and clipped areas have lighter shades of black. A small white spot on the chest is permitted, as is an occasional single white hair elsewhere on the body.

*Disqualifications* – Color solid white or white striping, patching, or spotting on the colored areas of the dog, except for the small white spot permitted on the chest of the black.

The body coat color in pepper and salt and black and silver dogs fades out to light gray or silver white under the throat and across the chest. Between them there exists a natural body coat color. Any irregular or connecting blaze or white mark in this section is considered a white patch on the body, which is also a disqualification.

*FCI*

Pure black with black undercoat.
Pepper and Salt.
Black/Silver.
Pure white with white undercoat.

When breeding Pepper and Salt, the aim is a medium shading with evenly distributed, well pigmented, pepper colouring and grey undercoat. The shades from dark iron grey to silver grey are all permitted. In all colour variations there must be a dark mask, which should adapt harmoniously to the respective colour. Distinct light markings on head, chest and limbs are undesirable.

For the Black/Silver colour, the aim in breeding is a black top coat with black undercoat, white markings over the eyes, on the cheeks, at the beard, at the throat, in two divided

In the US, a white Miniature Schnauzer would be disqualified.

triangles at the front of the chest, on the front pasterns, on the feet, on the inside of the hind legs and around the anus. The forehead, the neck and the outer sides of the ears should be black like the top coat.

The colours are well defined. White was first recognised by the FCI and has been recognised by the Kennel Club in the UK since November 2010. The AKC Breed Standard lists white as a disqualification. Significantly, the FCI stipulates that each colour is considered and treated as a completely separate breed. So there are no problems if other colours are added.

The distinctive pepper and salt is the most popular. This unique colouring comes about through the majority of grey hairs being banded dark-light-dark or light-dark-light, giving a colour range from dark steel through to a sterling silver. There are solid black and white hairs mixed in. It is important for the banded hairs to be in the majority and well defined, otherwise the coat will be blotchy, which is why "in even proportions" is included. The skin colour is grey.

Although not mentioned – but nevertheless important – are the dark hairs on the bridge of the nose, referred to as the dark mask. This helps give the 'down-the-nose' look, especially to the lighter greys. Through mixing of the colours, a clear difference between the pepper and salts and black and silver is not as marked as it should be. This is something that should be guarded against and thought about when considering matings.

The black and silver has a darker grey skin. The solid black colour pattern follows that of the pepper and salts, with no real grey or white hairs intermingled. With both pepper and salts and black and silvers, the main colour should come round the front of the neck, as there should not be an unbroken line of white under the chin and chest area.

The furnishings on both pepper and salts, and particularly the black and silvers, are becoming noticeably white and losing the correct silvery hue. If ignored, problems with pigmentation, skin texture and coat colour will follow.

Blacks should be a solid black, going right down to dark skin, along with a black, not dilute, undercoat. Except for a small white breast spot, there should be no intermingling white hairs. Whites are pure white with a white skin and undercoat. Pigment is black.

## FAULTS
### KC
**Any departure from the foregoing points should be**

# SIZE

### KC
**Ideal height: dogs 36 cms (14 inches); bitches: 33cms (13 inches). Too small, toyish appearing dogs are not typical and are undesirable.**

### AKC
**Size: From 12 to 14 inches. He is sturdily built, nearly square in proportion of body length to height with plenty of bone, and without any suggestion of toyishness. Disqualifications – Dogs or bitches under 12 inches or over 14 inches.**

### FCI
**Height at withers: Dogs and bitches between 30 and 35 cm. Weight: Dogs and bitches approximately 4 to 8 kg.**

Height is measured from the top of the shoulders (withers) to the ground. It is important to appreciate that a sturdy, robust Miniature in good coat will always appear bigger than their lighter bodied, finer boned counterpart.

Small and toyish being both untypical and undesirable reminds us of the intention for a small, sturdy dog having a job to do, not a pretty lap dog.

considered a fault, and the seriousness with which the fault should be regarded should be in exact proportion to its degree and the effect upon the health and welfare of the dog.

Note. Male animals should have two apparently normal testicles

fully descended into the scrotum.

## DISQUALIFICATIONS
### AKC
*Dogs or bitches under 12 inches or over 14 inches. Color solid white or white striping, patching, or spotting on the colored areas of the dog, except for the small white spot permitted on the chest of the black. The body coat color in pepper and salt and black and silver dogs fades out to light gray or silver white under the throat and across the chest. Between them there exists a natural body coat color. Any irregular or connecting blaze or white mark in this section is considered a white patch on the body, which is also a disqualification.*

### FCI
### FAULTS
**Any departure from the foregoing points should be considered a fault and the seriousness with which the fault should be regarded should be in exact proportion to its degree and its effect upon the health and welfare of the dog.**
**Particularly:**
**Heavy or round skull.**
**Wrinkles on forehead.**
**Short, pointed or narrow muzzle.**

Pincer bite.
Strongly protruding cheeks or cheekbones.
Light, too large or round eyes.
Low set, too long or unevenly carried ears.
Throatiness.
Dewlap, narrow crest or neck.
Too long, tucked up or soft back.
Roach back.
Croup falling away.
Tail set inclined towards head.
Long feet.
Pacing movement.
Too short, too long, soft, wavy, shaggy, silky coat.
Brown undercoat.
A black trace on the back or a black saddle.
In Black/Silver not clearly separated triangles on the chest.
Over- or undersize up to 1 cm.

### SERIOUS FAULTS
Clumsy or light build. Too low or too high on leg.
Inverse sexual type (e.g. doggy bitch).
Elbows turning out.
Straight or open hocked hindlegs.
Lower thigh too long.
Hocks turning inwards.
Rear pastern too short.
White or spotted coat in black or pepper and salt dogs.
Patchy coat in the colours black/silver and white.
Over- or undersize by more than 1 cm but less than 2 cm.

### DISQUALIFYING FAULTS
Shy, aggressive, vicious, exaggeratedly suspicious or

Breeders, exhibitors and judges bear a great responsibility to promote the breed in the best possible way, with health and temperament as absolute priorities.

nervous behaviour.
Malformation of any kind.
Lack of breed type.
Faulty mouth, such as over- or undershot or wry mouth.
Severe faults in individual parts, such as faults in construction, coat and colour.
Over- or undersize by more than 2 cm.

### KC
Any dog clearly showing physical or behavioural abnormalities shall be disqualified

NB: Male animals should have two apparently normal testicles fully descended into the scrotum.

The monorchid (one testicle) or the cryptorchid (none) can now be shown in Britain. However,

the generalised fault clause in the KC Standard does little, if anything, to draw attention to the breed's serious shortcomings, which need to be considered when judging or breeding.

The AKC Standard lists faults with the section headings and also stipulates disqualifications. The FCI Standard is very detailed in this area, with faults, serious faults and disqualifications carefully listed.

### SUMMING UP
A final thought is the importance for those who breed in any way – even those who only breed a single litter – to accept full responsibility, especially in relation to temperament and health. They must do their utmost for the breed, to ensure it is passed on in the best possible state to those who will follow.

# HAPPY AND HEALTHY

# Chapter 8

The Miniature Schnauzer is a breed with real character. They are such great fun, and find so much joy in life. They have a good life-span, which can run well into double figures, provided their needs are met. Like most breeds, the Miniature Schnauzer is renowned as a plucky, faithful companion and a willing friend on a non-conditional basis. He will, however, of necessity rely on you for food and shelter, accident prevention and medication. A healthy Miniature Schnauzer is a happy chap, looking to please and amuse his owner.

The Miniature Schnauzer does not shed his coat and may therefore be suitable to live in a household with someone who is allergic to dog fur.

There are only a few genetic conditions that have been recognised in the Miniature Schnauzer. They will be covered in depth later in the chapter.

## VACCINATION

There is much debate over the issue of vaccination at the moment. Timing of the final part of the initial vaccination course for a puppy and the frequency of subsequent booster vaccinations are both under scrutiny. An evaluation of the relative risk for each disease plays a part, depending on the local situation.

Many owners think that the actual vaccination is the protection, so that their puppy can go out for walks as soon as he or she has had the final part of the puppy vaccination course. This is not the case.

The rationale behind vaccination is to stimulate the immune system into producing protective antibodies that will be triggered if the patient is subsequently exposed to that particular disease. This means that a further one or two weeks will have to pass before an effective level of protection will have developed.

Vaccines against viruses stimulate longer lasting protection than those against bacteria, whose effect may only persist for a matter of months in some cases. There is also the possibility of an individual failing to mount a full immune response to a vaccination: although the vaccine schedule may have been followed as recommended, that particular dog remains vulnerable.

An individual's level of protection against rabies, as demonstrated by the antibody titre in a blood sample, is routinely tested in the UK in order to fulfil the requirements of the Pet Travel Scheme (PETS).

This is not the case with other individual diseases in order to gauge the need for booster vaccination or to determine the effect of a course of vaccines; instead, your veterinary surgeon will advise a protocol based upon the vaccines available, local disease prevalence, and the lifestyle of you and your dog.

It is worth remembering that maintaining a fully effective level of immune protection against the disease appropriate to your locale is vital: these are serious diseases, which may result in the demise of your dog, and some may have the potential to be passed on to his human family (so-called zoonotic potential for transmission). This is where you will be grateful for your veterinary surgeon's own knowledge and advice.

The American Animal Hospital Association laid down guidance at the end of 2006 for the vaccination of dogs in North America. Core diseases were defined as distemper, adenovirus, parvovirus and rabies. So-called non-core diseases are kennel cough, Lyme disease and leptospirosis; a decision to vaccinate against one or more non-core diseases will be based on an individual's level of risk, determined on lifestyle and where you live in the US.

Do remember, however, that the booster visit to the veterinary surgery is not 'just' for a booster. I am regularly correcting my clients when they announce that they have 'just' brought their pet for a booster. Instead, this appointment is a chance for a full health check and evaluation of how a particular dog is doing. After all, we are all conversant with the adage that a human year is equivalent to seven canine years.

There have been attempts in recent times to re-set the scale for two reasons: small breeds live longer than giant breeds, and dogs are living longer than previously. I have seen dogs of 17 and 18 years of age but to say a dog is 119 or 126 years old is plainly meaningless. It does emphasise the fact, though, that a dog's health can change dramatically over the course of a single year because dogs age at a far greater rate than humans.

For me as a veterinary surgeon, the booster vaccination visit is a challenge: how much can I find of which the owner was unaware, such as rotten teeth or a heart murmur? Even monitoring bodyweight year upon year is of use because bodyweight can creep up, or down, without an owner realising. Being overweight is unhealthy, but it may take an outsider's remark to make an owner realise that there is a problem. Conversely, a drop in bodyweight may be the only pointer to an underlying problem.

The diseases against which dogs are vaccinated include:

## ADENOVIRUS

Canine adenovirus 1 (CAV-1) affects the liver (hepatitis) and the classic 'blue eye' appearance in some affected dogs, whilst CAV-2 is a cause of kennel cough (see later). Vaccines often include both canine adenoviruses.

## CANINE PARVOVIRUS (CPV)

Canine parvovirus disease first appeared in the late 1970s when it was feared that the UK's dog population would be decimated by it because of the lack of immunity in the general canine

**Puppies receive their first immunity from their mother.**

**Kennel Cough will spread rapidly among dogs that live together.**

population. This was a notion that terrified me at the time but which did not fortunately happen on the scale envisaged.

There are two forms of the virus (CPV-1, CPV-2) affecting domesticated dogs. CPV-2 also affects wild dogs. The virus is highly contagious, picked up via the mouth/nose from infected faeces. The incubation period is about five days.

CPV-2 causes two types of illness: gastro-enteritis (vomiting, haemorrhagic diarrhoea, fever) and heart disease in puppies born to unvaccinated dams (myocarditis or inflammation of the cardiac muscle, heart failure, respiratory distress, diarrhoea), both of which often result in death.

Infection of puppies less than three weeks of age with CPV-1 manifests as diarrhoea, vomiting, difficulty breathing, and fading puppy syndrome. CPV-1 can

cause abortion and fetal abnormalities in breeding bitches.

Occurrence is mainly low now, thanks to vaccination against CPV-2. There is no vaccine available for CPV-1. The disease is more often mild or sub-clinical, with recovery more likely, although a recent outbreak in my area did claim the lives of several puppies and dogs. It is also occasionally seen in the elderly unvaccinated dog.

### DISTEMPER
This disease is also known as 'hardpad' from the characteristic changes to the pads of the paws. It has a worldwide distribution, but fortunately vaccination has been very effective at reducing its occurrence. It is caused by a virus and affects the respiratory, gastro-intestinal (gut) and nervous systems, so it causes a wide range of illnesses. Fox and urban stray dog populations are most at risk,

and therefore responsible for local outbreaks.

### KENNEL COUGH
Also known as **infectious tracheobronchitis**, *Bordetella bronchiseptica* is not only a major cause of kennel cough but also a common secondary infection on top of another cause. Being a bacterium, it is susceptible to treatment with appropriate antibiotics, but the immunity stimulated by the vaccine is therefore short-lived (six to 12 months).

This vaccine is often in a form to be administered down the nostrils in order to stimulate local immunity at the point of entry, so to speak. Do not be alarmed to see your veterinary surgeon using a needle and syringe to draw up the vaccine because the needle will be replaced with a special plastic introducer, allowing the vaccine to be gently instilled into each nostril. Dogs generally resent being held more than the actual intra-nasal vaccine, and I have learnt that covering the patient's eyes helps greatly.

Kennel cough is, however, rather a catch-all term for any cough spreading within a dog population not just in kennels but also between dogs at a training session or breed show, or even mixing out in the park. Many of these infections may not be *B. bronchiseptica* but other viruses, for which one can only treat symptomatically. **Parainfluenza** virus is often included in a vaccine programme because it is a common viral cause of kennel cough.

Kennel cough can seem alarming. There is a persistent cough accompanied by production of white frothy spittle, which can last for a matter of weeks, during which time the patient is highly infectious to other dogs. I remember when it ran through our five Border Collies – there were white patches of froth on the floor wherever you looked! Other features include sneezing, a runny nose, and eyes sore with conjunctivitis.

There are specific areas in the US where Lyme disease is prevalent.

Fortunately, these infections are generally self-limiting, most dogs recovering without any long-lasting problems, but an elderly dog may be knocked sideways by it, akin to the effects of a common cold on a frail elderly person.

## LYME DISEASE

This is a bacterial infection transmitted by hard ticks. It is It is restricted to those specific areas of the US where ticks are found, such as north-eastern states, some southern states, California and the upper Mississippi region. It does also occur in the UK but at a low level so vaccination is not routinely offered.

Clinical disease is manifested primarily as limping due to arthritis, but other organs affected include the heart, kidneys and nervous system. It is readily treatable with appropriate antibiotics, once diagnosed, but the causal bacterium, *Borrelia burgdorferi*, is not cleared from the body totally and will persist.

Prevention requires both vaccination and tick control, especially as there are other diseases transmitted by ticks. Ticks carrying *B. burgdorferi* will transmit it to humans as well, but an infected dog cannot pass it to a human.

## RABIES

This is another zoonotic disease and there are very strict control measures in place. Vaccines were once only available in the UK on an individual basis for dogs being taken abroad. Pets travelling into the UK had to serve six months' compulsory quarantine so that any pet incubating rabies would be identified before release back into the general population. Under the Pet Travel Scheme, provided certain criteria are met (and I would refer you to the DEFRA website for up-to-date

# LEPTOSPIROSIS

Disease is caused by *Leptospira interogans*, a spiral-shaped bacterium. There are several natural variants or serovars. Each is characteristically found in one or more particular host animal species, which then acts as a reservoir, intermittently shedding leptospires in the urine. Infection can also be picked up at mating, via bite wounds, across the placenta, or through eating the carcases of infected animals, such as rats.

A serovar will cause actual clinical disease in an individual when two conditions are fulfilled: the individual is not the natural host species, and is also not immune to that particular serovar.

Leptospirosis is a zoonotic disease, known as Weil's disease in humans, with implications for all those in contact with an affected dog. It is also commonly called rat jaundice, reflecting the rat's important role as a reservoir of *Leptospira icterohaemorrhagiae* to both humans and dogs. Wherever you live in the UK, rats are endemic, meaning that there is as much a risk for the Miniature Schnauzer living with a family in a town as the Miniature Schnauzer leading a rural lifestyle.

Signs of illness reflect the organs affected by a particular serovar. In man, there may be a flu-like illness or a more serious, often life-threatening disorder involving major body organs.

The illness in a susceptible dog may be mild, the dog recovering within two to three weeks without treatment but going on to develop long-term liver or kidney disease. In contrast, peracute illness may result in a rapid deterioration and death following initial malaise and fever. There may also be anorexia, vomiting, diarrhoea, abdominal pain, joint pain, increased thirst and rate of urination, jaundice, and ocular changes. Haemorrhage is a common feature because of low platelet numbers, manifesting as bleeding under the skin, nose-bleeds (epistaxis), and the presence of blood in the urine and faeces (haematuria and melaena respectively).

Treatment requires rigorous intravenous fluid therapy to support the kidneys. Being a bacterial infection, it is possible to treat leptospirosis with specific antibiotics, although a prolonged course of several weeks is needed. Strict hygiene and barrier nursing are required in order to avoid onward transmission of the disease.

Annual vaccination is recommended for leptospirosis because the immunity only lasts for a year, unlike the longer immunity associated with vaccines against viruses. There is, however, little or no cross-protection between *Leptospira* serovars, so vaccination will result in protection against only those serovars included in the particular vaccine used. Additionally, although vaccination against leptospirosis will prevent active disease if an individual is exposed to a serovar included in the vaccine, it cannot prevent infection of that individual and becoming a carrier in the long-term.

In the UK, vaccines have classically included *L icterohaemorrhagiae* (rat-adapted serovar) and *L canicola* (dog-specific serovar). The latter is of especial significance to us humans, since disease will not be apparent in an infected dog but leptospires will be shed intermittently.

information – www.defra.gov.uk) then dogs can re-enter the UK without being quarantined.

Dogs to be imported into the US have to show that they were vaccinated against rabies at least 30 days previously; otherwise, they have to serve effective internal quarantine for 30 days from the date of vaccination against rabies, in order to ensure they are not incubating rabies. The exception is dogs entering from countries recognised as being rabies-free, in which case it has to be proved that they lived in that country for at least six months beforehand.

## PARASITES

A parasite is defined as an organism deriving benefit on a one-way basis from another, the host. It goes without saying that it is not to the parasite's advantage to harm the host to such an extent that the benefit is lost, especially if it results in the death of the host.

This means a dog could harbour parasites, internal and/or external, without there being any signs apparent to the owner. Many canine parasites can, however, transfer to humans with variable consequences, so routine preventative treatment is advised against particular parasites. Just as with vaccination, risk assessment plays a part – for example, there is no need for routine heartworm treatment in the UK (at present), but it is vital in the US and in Mediterranean countries.

## ROUNDWORMS (NEMATODES)

These are the spaghetti-like worms, which you may have been unfortunate enough to have seen passed in faeces or brought up in vomit. Most of the de-worming treatments in use today cause the adult roundworms to disintegrate, thankfully, so that treating puppies in particular is not as unpleasant as it used to be!

Most puppies will have a worm burden, mainly of a particular roundworm species (*Toxocara canis*) which reactivates within the dam's tissues during pregnancy and passes to the foetuses developing in the womb. It is therefore important to treat the dam both during and after pregnancy, as well as the puppies.

Professional advice is to continue worming every one to three months. There are roundworm eggs in the environment and, unless you examine your dog's faeces under a microscope on a very regular basis for the presence of roundworm eggs, you will be unaware of your dog having picked up roundworms, unless he should have such a heavy burden that he passes the adults.

It takes a few weeks from the time that a dog swallows a *Toxocara canis* roundworm egg to himself passing viable eggs (the pre-patent period). These eggs are not immediately infective to other animals, requiring a period of

**You will need to continue the worming programme started by your puppy's breeder.**

# TAPEWORMS (CESTODES)

When considering the general dog population, the primary source of the commonest tapeworm species will be fleas, which can carry the eggs. Most multi-wormers will be active against these tapeworms, not because they are a hazard to human health but because it is unpleasant to see the wriggly rice grain tapeworm segments emerging from your dog's back passage whilst he is lying in front of the fire, and usually when you have had guests for dinner.

A tapeworm of significance to human health is Echinococcus granulosus, found in a few parts of the UK, mainly in Wales. Humans are an intermediate host for this tapeworm, along with sheep, cattle and pigs. Inadvertent ingestion of eggs passed in the faeces of an infected dog is followed by the development of so-called hydatid cysts in major organs, such as the lungs and liver, necessitating surgical removal. Dogs become infected through eating raw meat containing hydatid cysts. Cooking will kill hydatid cysts, so the general advice is to avoid feeding raw meat and offal in areas of high risk. There are specific requirements for treatment with praziquantel within 24 to 48 hours of return into the UK under the PETS. This is to prevent the inadvertent introduction of Echinococcus multilocularis, a tapeworm carried by foxes on mainland Europe, which is transmissible to humans, causing serious or even fatal liver disease.

maturation in the environment, which is primarily temperature dependent and therefore shorter in the summer (as little as two weeks) than in the winter (several months). It is worth noting that the eggs can survive in the environment for two years and more.

There are de-worming products that are active all the time, which will provide continuous protection when administered as often as directed. Otherwise, treating every month will, in effect, cut in before a dog could theoretically become a source of roundworm eggs to the general population.

It is the risk to human health that is so important: *T. canis* roundworms will migrate within our tissues and cause all manner of problems, not least of which (but fortunately rarely) is blindness. The incidence in humans has fallen dramatically in recent years. If a dog has roundworms, the eggs also find their way on to his coat where they can be picked up during stroking and cuddling. Sensible hygiene is therefore important.

You should always carefully pick up your dog's faeces and dispose of them appropriately, thereby preventing the maturation of any eggs present in the fresh faeces.

This will not only reduce the chance for environmental contamination with all manner of infections but also make walking more pleasant underfoot.

## HEARTWORM (DIROFILARIA IMMITIS)

Heartworm infection has been diagnosed in dogs all over the world. There are two prerequisites: presence of mosquitoes, and a warm humid climate.

When a female mosquito bites an infected animal, it acquires *D. immitis* in its circulating form, as microfilariae. A warm environmental temperature is needed for these microfilariae to develop into the infective third-stage larvae (L3) within the mosquitoes, the so-called intermediate host. L3 larvae are then transmitted by the mosquito when it next bites a dog. Therefore, while heartworm infection is found in all the states of the US, it is at differing levels such that an occurrence in Alaska, for example, is probably a reflection of a visiting dog having previously picked up the infection elsewhere.

Heartworm infection is not currently a problem in the UK, except for those dogs contracting it while abroad without suitable preventative treatment. Global warming and its effect on the UK's climate, however, could change that.

It is a potentially life-threatening condition, with dogs of all breeds and ages being susceptible without preventative treatment. The larvae can grow to 14 inches within the right side of the heart, causing primarily signs of heart failure and ultimately liver and kidney damage. It can be treated, but prevention is a better plan. In the US, regular blood tests for the presence of infection are advised, coupled with appropriate preventative measures, so I would advise liaison with your veterinary surgeon.

For dogs travelling to

**Daily grooming will ensure that you spot any sign of external parasites.**

heartworm-endemic areas of the EU, such as the Mediterranean coast, preventative treatment should be started before leaving the UK and maintained during the visit. Again, this is best arranged with your veterinary surgeon.

### FLEAS

There are several species of flea, which are not host-specific: not only can a dog be carrying cat and human fleas as well as dog fleas, but also the same flea treatment will kill and/or control them all. It is also accepted that environmental control is a vital

part of a flea control programme. This is because the adult flea is only on the animal for as long as it takes to have a blood meal and to breed; the remainder of the life cycle occurs in the house, car, caravan, shed...

There is a vast array of flea control products available, with various routes of administration: collar, powder, spray, 'spot-on', or oral. Since flea control needs to be applied to all pets in the house, and that is independent of whether they leave the house (since fleas can be introduced into the house by other pets and their human owners), it is best to discuss your specific flea control needs with your veterinary surgeon.

### MITES

There are five types of mite that can affect dogs:

**Demodex canis:** This mite is a normal inhabitant of canine hair follicles, passed from the bitch to her pups as they suckle. The development of actual skin disease or **demodicosis** depends on the individual. It is seen frequently around the time of puberty and after a bitch's first season, associated with hormonal changes. There may, however, be an inherited weakness in an individual's immune system, enabling multiplication of the mite. The localised form consists of areas of fur loss without itchiness, generally around the face and on the forelimbs, and 90 per cent will recover without treatment.

The other 10 per cent develop the juvenile-onset generalised form, of which half will recover spontaneously. The other half may be depressed, go off their food, and show signs of itchiness due to secondary bacterial skin infections. Treatment is often prolonged over several months and consists of regular bathing with a specific miticidal shampoo, often clipping away fur to improve access to the skin, together with a suitable antibiotic by mouth. There is also now a licensed 'spot-on' preparation available. Progress is monitored by examination of deep skin scrapings for the presence of the mite; the initial diagnosis is based upon abnormally high numbers of the mite, often with live individuals being seen.

There is a third group of individuals developing demodicosis for the first time in middle-age (more than about four years of age), and as the generalised form. This is often reflecting underlying immunosuppression by an internal disease process, such as neoplasia, or treatment with corticosteroids, for example, so it is important to identify any predisposing cause and correct it where possible, as well as specifically treating as above.

*Sarcoptes scabei:* This characteristically causes an intense pruritus or itchiness in the affected dog, causing the dog to incessantly scratch and bite at himself, leading to marked fur loss and skin trauma. Initially starting on the elbows, ear flaps and hocks, without treatment the skin on the rest of the body can become involved, with thickening and pigmentation of the skin. Secondary bacterial infections are common.

Unlike *Demodex*, this mite lives at the skin surface, and it can be hard to find in skin scrapings. It is therefore not unusual to treat a patient for **sarcoptic mange (scabies)** based on the appearance of the problem even with negative skin scraping findings, and especially if there is a history of contact with foxes, which are a frequent source of the scabies mite. It will spread between dogs and can therefore also be found in situations where large numbers of dogs from different backgrounds are mixing together. It should be noted that it will cause itchiness in humans, although the mite cannot complete its life cycle on us, so treating all

affected dogs should be sufficient.

Fortunately, there is now a highly effective 'spot-on' treatment for *Sarcoptes scabei*.

*Cheyletiella yasguri:* This is the fur mite most commonly found on dogs. It is often called **'walking dandruff'** because it can be possible to see collections of the small white mite moving about over the skin surface. There is excessive scale and dandruff formation, and mild itchiness. It is important as a zoonosis, being

**Keep a close check in the ears for evidence of infection.**

transmissible to humans, where it causes a pruritic rash.

Diagnosis is by microscopic examination of skin scrapings, coat combings and sticky tape impressions from the skin and fur. Treatment is with an appropriate insecticide, as advised by your veterinary surgeon.

**Otodectes cynotis:** A highly transmissible otitis externa (outer ear infection) results from the presence in the outer ear canal of this ear mite, characterised by exuberant production of dark earwax. The patient will frequently shake his head and rub at the ear(s) affected. The mites can also spread on to the skin adjacent to the opening of the

external ear canal, and may transfer elsewhere, such as to the paws.

When using an otoscope to examine the outer ear canal, the heat from the light source will often cause any ear mites present to start moving around. I often offer owners the chance to have a look because it really is quite an extraordinary sight! It is also possible to identify the mite from ear wax smeared on to a slide and examined under a microscope.

Cats are a common source of ear mites. It is not unusual to find ear mites during the routine examination of puppies and kittens. Treatment options include specific ear drops acting against both the mite and any secondary

infections present in the auditory canal, and certain 'spot-on' formulations. It is vital to treat all dogs and cats in the household to prevent re-cycling of the mite between individuals.

**(Neo-) Trombicula autumnalis:** The free-living harvest mite can cause an intense local irritation on the skin. Its larvae are picked up from undergrowth, so they are characteristically found as a bright orange patch on the web of skin between the digits of the paws. It feeds on skin cells before dropping off to complete its life cycle in the environment.

Its name is a little misleading because it is not restricted to the autumn nor to harvest-time; I find

# TICKS

Ticks have become an increasing problem in recent years throughout Britain. Their physical presence causes irritation, but it is their potential to spread disease that causes concern. A tick will transmit any infection previously contracted while feeding on an animal: for example Borrelia burgdorferi, the causal agent of Lyme disease (see page 132).

The life cycle of the tick is curious: each life stage takes a year to develop and move on to the next. Long grass is a major habitat. The vibration of animals moving through the grass will stimulate the larva, nymph or adult to climb up a blade of grass and wave its legs in the air

as it 'quests' for a host on to which to latch for its next blood meal. Humans are as likely to be hosts, so ramblers and orienteers are advised to cover their legs when going through rough long grass.

Removing a tick is simple – provided your dog will stay still. The important rule is to twist gently so that the tick is persuaded to let go with its mouthparts. Grasp the body of the tick as near to your dog's skin as possible, either between thumb and fingers or with a specific tick-removing instrument, and then rotate in one direction until the tick comes away. I keep a plastic tick hook in my wallet at all times.

**The responsible owner should acquire a basic knowledge of canine ailments.**

it on the ear flaps of cats from late June onwards, depending on the prevailing weather. It will also bite humans.

Treatment depends on identifying and avoiding hotspots for picking up harvest mite, if possible. Checking the skin, especially the paws, after exercise and mechanically removing any mites found will reduce the chances of irritation, which can be treated symptomatically. Insecticides can also be applied – be guided by your veterinary surgeon.

## A-Z OF COMMON AILMENTS

### ANAL SACS (IMPACTED)
The anal sacs lie on either side of the back passage or anus at approximately four- and eight-o'-

clock, if compared with the face of a clock. They fill with a particularly pungent fluid, which is emptied on to the faeces as they move past the sacs to exit from the anus. Theories abound as to why these sacs should become impacted periodically and seemingly more so in some dogs than others. The irritation of impacted anal sacs is often seen as 'scooting', when the backside is dragged along the ground. Some dogs will gnaw at their back feet or over the rump.

Increasing the fibre content of the diet helps some dogs; in others, there is underlying skin disease. It may be a one-off occurrence for no apparent reason. Sometimes, an infection can become established, requiring antibiotic therapy, which may need to be coupled with flushing

out the infected sac under sedation or general anaesthesia. More rarely, a dog will present with an apparently acute-onset anal sac abscess, which is incredibly painful.

### DIARRHOEA
Cause and treatment much as **G**astritis (see below).

### EAR INFECTIONS
The dog has a long external ear canal, initially vertical then horizontal, leading to the eardrum, which protects the middle ear. If your Miniature Schnauzer is shaking his head, then his ears will need to be inspected with an auroscope by a veterinary surgeon in order to identify any cause, and to ensure the eardrum is intact. A sample may be taken from the canal to be

141

# FOREIGN BODIES

**Internal:** Items swallowed in haste without checking whether they will be digested can cause problems if they lodge in the stomach or obstruct the intestines, necessitating surgical removal. Acute vomiting is the main indication. Common objects I have seen removed include stones from the garden, peach stones, babies' dummies, golf balls, and once a lady's bra ...

It is possible to diagnose a dog with an intestinal obstruction across a waiting room from a particularly 'tucked-up' stance and pained facial expression. These patients bounce back from surgery dramatically. A previously docile and compliant obstructed patient will return for a post-operative check-up and literally bounce into the consulting room.

**External:** Grass awns are adept at finding their way into orifices such as a nostril, down an ear, and into the soft skin between two digits (toes), whence they start a one-way journey due to the direction of their whiskers. In particular, I remember a grass awn that migrated from a hindpaw, causing abscesses along the way but not yielding itself up until it erupted through the skin in the groin!

examined under the microscope and cultured to identify causal agents before prescribing appropriate ear drops containing antibiotic, anti-fungal agent and/or steroid. Predisposing causes of otitis externa or infection in the external ear canal include:

- Presence of a foreign body, such as a grass awn
- Ear mites, which are intensely irritating to the dog and stimulate the production of brown wax, predisposing to infection
- Previous infections, causing the canal's lining to thicken, narrowing the canal and reducing ventilation
- Swimming – if your Miniature Schnauzer does like swimming, do bear in mind that water trapped in the external ear canal can lead to infection, especially if the water is not clean! Equally, take care when bathing him.

## GASTRITIS

This is usually a simple stomach upset, most commonly in response to dietary indiscretion. Scavenging constitutes a change in the diet as much as an abrupt switch in the food being fed by the owner. There are also some specific infections causing more severe gastritis/enteritis, which will require treatment from a veterinary surgeon (See also **Canine Parvovirus** under 'Vaccination' earlier).

Generally, a day without food followed by a few days of small, frequent meals of a bland diet, such as cooked chicken or fish or an appropriate prescription diet, should allow the stomach to settle. It is vital to ensure the patient is drinking and retaining sufficient to cover losses resulting from the stomach upset in addition to the normal losses to be expected when healthy. Oral rehydration fluid may not be very appetising for the patient, in which case cooled boiled water should be offered. Fluids should initially be offered in small but frequent amounts to avoid over-drinking, which can result in further vomiting and thereby dehydration and electrolyte imbalances.

It is also important to gradually wean the patient back on to routine food or else another bout of gastritis may occur.

## JOINT PROBLEMS

It is not unusual for older Miniature Schnauzers to be stiff after exercise, particularly in cold weather. Your veterinary surgeon will be able to advise you on ways for helping your dog cope with stiffness, not least of which will be to ensure that he is not overweight. Arthritic joints do not need to be burdened with extra bodyweight!

## LUMPS AND BUMPS

Regularly handling and stroking your dog will enable the early detection of lumps and bumps. These may be due to infection (abscess), bruising, multiplication of particular cells from within the body, or even an external parasite (tick). If you are worried about any lump you find, have it checked by a veterinary surgeon.

## OBESITY

Being overweight does predispose to many other problems, such as **diabetes mellitus, heart disease** and **joint problems**. It is so easily prevented by simply acting as your Miniature Schnauzer's conscience. Ignore pleading eyes and feed according to your dog's waistline. The body condition is what matters qualitatively, alongside monitoring that individual's bodyweight as a quantitative measure. The

**Scavenging is a common cause of gastric upset.**

Miniature Schnauzer should, in my opinion as a health professional, have at least a suggestion of a waist and it should be possible to feel the ribs beneath only a slight layer of fat.

Neutering does not automatically mean that your Miniature Schnauzer will be overweight. Having an ovario-hysterectomy does slow down the body's rate of working, castration to a lesser extent, but it therefore means that your dog needs less food, a lower energy intake. I recommend cutting back a little on the amount of food fed a few weeks before neutering to accustom your Miniature Schnauzer to less food. If she looks a little underweight on the

morning of the operation, it will help the veterinary surgeon as well as giving her a little leeway weight-wise afterwards.

It is always harder to lose weight after neutering than before, because of this slowing in the body's inherent metabolic rate.

## TEETH PROBLEMS

Eating food starts with the canine teeth gripping and killing prey in the wild, incisor teeth biting off pieces of food and the molar teeth chewing it. To be able to eat is vital for life, yet the actual health of the teeth is often over-looked: unhealthy teeth can predispose to disease, and not just by reducing the ability to eat. The presence of infection within the mouth can lead to bacteria entering the bloodstream and then filtering out at major organs, with the potential for serious consequences. That is not to forget that simply having dental pain can affect a dog's well-being, as anyone who has had toothache will confirm.

Veterinary dentistry has made huge leaps in recent years, so that it no longer consists of extraction as the treatment of necessity.

Good dental health lies in the hands of the owner, starting from the moment the dog comes into your care. Just as we have taken on responsibility for feeding, so we have acquired the task of maintaining good dental and oral hygiene. In an ideal world, we should brush our dogs' teeth as regularly as our own. The Miniature Schnauzer puppy who finds having his teeth brushed is a huge game and an excuse to roll over and over on the ground requires loads of patience, twice a day.

There are alternative strategies, ranging from dental chew-sticks to specially formulated foods, but the main thing is to be aware of your dog's mouth. At least train your puppy to permit full examination of his teeth, which will not only ensure you are checking in his mouth regularly but also make your veterinary surgeon's job easier when there is a real need for your dog to, "Open wide!"

## INHERITED DISORDERS

Any individual, dog or human, may have an inherited disorder by virtue of genes acquired from the parents. This is significant not only for the health of that individual but also because of the potential for transmitting the disorder on to that individual's offspring and to subsequent generations, depending on the mode of inheritance.

There are control schemes in place for some inherited disorders. In the US, for example, the Canine Eye Registration

Foundation (CERF) was set up by dog breeders concerned about heritable eye disease, and provides a database of dogs who have been examined by diplomates of the American College of Veterinary Ophthalmologists.

Very few inherited conditions have been confirmed in the Miniature Schnauzer, and are primarily to do with the eyes (see page 41 for additional information about testing). These include:

- **Hereditary cataract**: A cataract is a cloudiness of the lens of the eye. Two forms of inherited cataract have been recognised in the Miniature Schnauzer. The congenital form is inherited as an autosomal recessive trait; puppies can be assessed for it at six to eight weeks old. The developmental form of hereditary cataract occurs in the young or middle-aged dog and can be diagnosed from six months of age. They are controlled under Schedule A of the BVA/KC/ISDS Scheme* in

**Breeders strive to eliminate inherited disorders from their breeding programmes.**

the UK, CERF in the US.

• **Retinal defects**: Generalised or late-onset progressive retinal atrophy is controlled under Schedule A of the BVA/KC/ISDS Scheme* in the UK. It may be not be apparent until two to three years of age at the earliest.

The Miniature Schnauzer seems to be predisposed to two forms of congenital heart abnormalities: patent ductus arteriosus and pulmonic stenosis. There may also be a predisposition to developing two forms of heart problem later in life: endocardiosis and sick sinus syndrome.

\* British Veterinary Association/Kennel Club/International Sheepdog Society Scheme

• **Haemophilia A –** Haemophilia is the most common disorder of blood coagulation, inherited in a sex-linked recessive fashion. This means that the male is either affected or clear, whilst females can alternatively be carriers for the trait. Haemophilia A arises from a deficiency of blood-clotting Factor VIII.

There are many ways in which haemophilia A can manifest, at worst as sudden death. There may be early indications, such as prolonged bleeding when the baby teeth are lost or unexpected bruising under the skin. A problem may not become apparent until after surgery, such as routine neutering or an injury. Treatment will often require a blood transfusion.

## SUMMARY

As the owner of a Miniature Schnauzer, you are responsible for his care and health. Not only must you make decisions on his behalf, you are also responsible for establishing a lifestyle for him which that will ensure he leads a long and happy life.

It is important to remember that your Miniature Schnauzer has no choice. As his owner, you are responsible for any decision made, so it must be as informed a decision as possible. Always speak to your veterinary surgeon if you have any concerns about your Miniature Schnauzer. After all, he isn't just a dog; he became a member of the family from the moment you brought him home.

**With good care and management, your Miniature Schnauzer should live a long, happy and healthy life.**

# THE CONTRIBUTORS

**THE EDITOR:**
## JUDY CHILDERLEY (CHILDGAIT)

Judy grew up in a Gloucestershire village and always had dogs and horses around her. Working as a groom in the Beaufort country started her career with horses, and she always had a dog in tow. Her main involvement was with training gundogs, and it was through one of her gundog owners that she first discovered Miniature Schnauzers. She met a dog called Mable and was smitten from the first touch. Judy decided she had to have one.

Molly, her first Miniature Schnauzer was good enough to show and Judy enjoyed competing in open shows. Molly was her foundation bitch, and along came Milly, Mable and Maud.

Going to the top stud dogs gave Judy the opportunity to be successful in the show ring and her third generation, called Maud, had two Best Puppy in the Breed at Championship shows the same year. Sadly, health problems meant that Judy has to curtail her showing career but she has concentrated on producing top quality Miniature Schnauzers which have made a lot of owners very happy.

She says: "Over the last twenty years I have had so much fun and enjoyment with these little dogs, I know I could never be without one. One word of warning: They grow on you…"
*See Chapter One: Getting to Know Miniature Schnauzers; Chapter Four: The New Arrival; Chapter Seven: The Perfect Miniature Schnauzer.*

## KIRSTY SANDERS (ZAKMAYO)

Kirsty started showing Dobermans as a child and the Zakmayo Kennel is a partnership between Kirsty and her mother, Vivien. At a show one day, a Miniature Schnauzer caught their eye and so began their quest to find their first show Miniature Schnauzer.

From experience they knew that to succeed in the ring and as breeders (particularly in a new breed), they needed to start with the best quality stock they could find. After studying the show dogs around at that time, they finally bought their first Miniature Schnauzer from Roger and Elaine Ward of the Wrendras Kennel in 1991.

There then followed a very steep learning curve, especially regarding grooming. Twenty-something years on, Kirsty is still delighted when she realises that if she does 'it' slightly differently she get a whole new look!

Over the years, Zakmayo has had considerable success producing many champions in both the UK and Ireland. Zakmayo Miniature Schanuzers have gained (on numerous occasions) Top Miniature Schnauzer, Top Miniature Schnauzer Dog, Top

Miniature Schnauzer Bitch, Top Miniature Schnauzer Brood Bitch, Top Miniature Schnauzer Kennel and have won the Dog CC, the Bitch CC and Best Puppy at Crufts, with both Best of Breed and Best Opposite Sex.

To date, a very special dog for Kirsty, is Ch ToMar's Two Thumbs Up to Zakmayo (Sizzle) which was imported from Mary Paisley of the ToMar Kennel in Wisconsin, USA. Sizzle is a Multi Group winner and placer at Major Championship Shows, where the entry is often greater than 10,000 dogs, plus a Best in Show winner for three consecutive years at The Miniature Schnauzer Club Championship Show. Sizzle is also proving himself as a sire and has taken Zakmayo's breeding programme onto a completely new course.

Kirsty says, "After buying our first Mini, never did we think that it would completely take over our lives in the way in which it has....beware! it could happen to you too…"
*See Chapter Three: A Miniature Schnauzer for your Lifestyle; Chapter Five: The Best of Care.*

## PETER NEWMAN (RISEPARK)

Peter Newman has been completely devoted to Miniature Schnauzers since 1955, when he started out with a daughter of Champion Deltone Appeline Doughboy. Since 1985 he has been in partnership with Barry Day.

Keeping to the pepper and salt colour, Peter and Barry's breeding programme centres on American bloodlines and their imports have played a major part in the breed's development and progress in Britain.

Risepark has proven successful at the highest level at general Championship breed shows, as well as national All Breed sponsored stakes. It is a name known and respected throughout the world. It has also set many firsts for the breed, including the first British-bred Miniature Champion to also become an American Champion.
*See Chapter Two: The First Miniature Schnauzers; Chapter Seven: The Perfect Miniature Schnauzer.*

## JULIA BARNES

Julia has owned and trained a number of different dog breeds, and has also worked as a puppy socialiser for Dogs for the Disabled. A former journalist, she has written many books, including several on dog training and behaviour. Julia is indebted to Judy Childerley for her specialist knowledge about Miniature Schnauzers.
*See Chapter Six: Training and Socialisation.*

## ALISON LOGAN MA VetMB MRCVS

Alison qualified as a veterinary surgeon from Cambridge University in 1989, having been brought up surrounded by all manner of

animals and birds in the north Essex countryside. She has been in practice in her home town ever since, living with her husband, two children and Labrador Retriever Pippin.

She contributes on a regular basis to *Veterinary Times, Veterinary Nurse Times, Dogs Today, Cat World* and *Pet Patter*, the PetPlan newsletter. In 1995, Alison won the Univet Literary Award with an article on Cushing's Disease, and she won it again (as the Vetoquinol Literary Award) in 2002, writing about common conditions in the Shar-Pei.
*See Chapter Eight: Happy and Healthy.*

## US CONTRIBUTORS

## MARCY ZINGLER (US CONSULTANT)

Marcy L. Zingler was Senior Editor at Howell Book House before joining the AKC staff as Corporate Project Manager. One of her primary responsibilities was as Project Editor for the award-winning AKC 125th Anniversary book. As a freelancer, she was the only outside editor to work on *The AKC Complete Dog Book*, 20th Edition and 19th Revised.

Marcy's forty-year participation in the dog sport has included breeding, exhibiting, judging, and active leadership in national clubs as officeholder, AKC Delegate and Judges' Education Chair. A three-time National Specialty judge in her original breed, other assignments have included the AKC Eukanuba National Championship in addition to judging overseas and across the US.

Now semi-retired, in addition to judging, she again serves as a Delegate to the American Kennel Club.

## WYOMA CLOUSS

Wyoma Clouss, a retired speech pathologist, entered the world of Miniature Schnauzers in 1974. After a professional handler finished their first four champions, Wyoma and Owen Clouss finished their next 33 owner/handled, all but 3 also bred by them. Wyoma served four terms as American Miniature Schnauzer Club (AMSC) President, is again serving on the AMSC Board of Directors, and is the current AMSC Judges Education Chair.

She also has been President, Show Chair, and Board Member of the Idaho Capital City Kennel Club, and serves as their AKC Delegate. She is approved to judge the Terrier Group, and four Working breeds. Wyoma has had the honour of judging the American Miniature Schnauzer Club National Specialty 3 times; 1997, 2003, and at Montgomery County in 2007.

# USEFUL ADDRESSES

## KENNEL & BREED CLUBS

### UK
**The Kennel Club**
1-5 Clarges Street, London, W1J 8AB
Tel: 0870 606 6750
Fax: 0207 518 1058
Web: www.the-kennel-club.org.uk

To obtain up-to-date contact information for the following breed clubs, contact the Kennel Club:
• Miniature Schnauzer Club
• Northern Schnauzer Club
• Schnauzer Club of Great Britain

### USA
**American Kennel Club (AKC)**
5580 Centerview Drive,
Raleigh, NC 27606, USA.
Tel: 919 233 9767
Fax: 919 233 3627
Email: info@akc.org
Web: www.akc.org

**United Kennel Club (UKC)**
100 E Kilgore Rd, Kalamazoo,
MI 49002-5584, USA.
Tel: 269 343 9020
Fax: 269 343 7037
Web:www.ukcdogs.com/

**The American Miniature Schnauzer Club, Inc.**
Web: http://amsc.us/

For contact details of regional clubs, please contact The American Miniature Schnauzer Club.

### AUSTRALIA
**Australian National Kennel Council (ANKC)**
The Australian National Kennel Council is the administrative body for pure breed canine affairs in Australia. It does not, however, deal directly with dog exhibitors, breeders or judges. For information pertaining to breeders, clubs or shows, please contact the relevant State or Territory Controlling Body.

**Dogs Australian Capital Teritory**
PO Box 815, Dickson ACT 2602
Tel: (02) 6241 4404
Fax: (02) 6241 1129
Email: administrator@dogsact.org.au
Web: www.dogsact.org.au

**Dogs New South Wales**
PO Box 632, St Marys, NSW 1790
Tel: (02) 9834 3022 or 1300 728 022 (NSW Only)
Fax: (02) 9834 3872
Email: info@dogsnsw.org.au
Web: www.dogsnsw.org.au

**Dogs Northern Territory**
PO Box 37521, Winnellie NT 0821
Tel: (08) 8984 3570
Fax: (08) 8984 3409
Email: admin@dogsnt.com.au
Web: www.dogsnt.com.au

**Dogs Queensland**
PO Box 495, Fortitude Valley Qld 4006
Tel: (07) 3252 2661
Fax: (07) 3252 3864
Email: info@dogsqueensland.org.au
Web: www.dogsqueensland.org.au

**Dogs South Australia**
PO Box 844
Prospect East SA 5082
Tel: (08) 8349 4797
Fax: (08) 8262 5751
Email: info@dogssa.com.au
Web: www.dogssa.com.au

**Tasmanian Canine Association Inc**
The Rothman Building
PO Box 116
Glenorchy Tas 7010
Tel: (03) 6272 9443
Fax: (03) 6273 0844
Email: tca@iprimus.com.au
Web: www.tasdogs.com

**Dogs Victoria**
Locked Bag K9
Cranbourne VIC 3977
Tel: (03)9788 2500
Fax: (03) 9788 2599
Email: office@dogsvictoria.org.au
Web: www.dogsvictoria.org.au

**Dogs Western Australia**
PO Box 1404
Canning Vale WA 6970
Tel: (08) 9455 1188
Fax: (08) 9455 1190
Email: k9@dogswest.com
Web: www.dogswest.com

### INTERNATIONAL
**Fédération Cynologique Internationalé (FCI)/World Canine Organisation**
Place Albert 1er, 13, B-6530 Thuin, Belgium.
Tel: +32 71 59.12.38
Fax: +32 71 59.22.29
Web: www.fci.be/

## TRAINING AND BEHAVIOUR

### UK
**Association of Pet Dog Trainers**
PO Box 17, Kempsford, GL7 4WZ
Telephone: 01285 810811
Email: APDToffice@aol.com
Web: http://www.apdt.co.uk

**Association of Pet Behaviour Counsellors**
PO BOX 46, Worcester, WR8 9YS
Telephone: 01386 751151
Fax: 01386 750743
Email: info@apbc.org.uk
Web: http://www.apbc.org.uk/

### USA
**Association of Pet Dog Trainers**
101 North Main Street, Suite 610
Greenville, SC 29601, USA.
Tel: 1 800 738 3647
Email: information@apdt.com
Web: www.apdt.com/

**American College of Veterinary Behaviorists**
College of Veterinary Medicine, 4474 Tamu,
Texas A&M University
College Station, Texas 77843-4474
Web: http://dacvb.org/

**American Veterinary Society of Animal Behavior**
Web: www.avsabonline.org/

### AUSTRALIA
**APDT Australia Inc**
PO Box 3122, Bankstown Square, NSW 2200,
Email: secretary@apdt.com.au
Web: www.apdt.com.au

**Canine Behaviour**
For details of regional behvaiourists, contact the relevant State or Territory Controlling Body.

## ACTIVITIES

### UK
**Agility Club**
http://www.agilityclub.co.uk/

**British Flyball Association**
PO Box 990, Doncaster, DN1 9FY
Telephone: 01628 829623
Email: secretary@flyball.org.uk
Web: http://www.flyball.org.uk/

### USA
**North American Dog Agility Council**
P.O. Box 1206, Colbert,
OK 74733, USA.
Web: www.nadac.com/

**North American Flyball Association, Inc.**
1333 West Devon Avenue, #512
Chicago, IL 60660
Tel/Fax: 800 318 6312
Email: flyball@flyball.org
Web: www.flyball.org/

**Agility Dog Association of Australia**
ADAA Secretary, PO Box 2212,
Gailes, QLD 4300, Australia.
Tel: 0423 138 914
Email: admin@adaa.com.au
Web: www.adaa.com.au/

**NADAC Australia (North American Dog Agility Council - Australian Division)**
12 Wellman Street, Box Hill South, Victoria 3128, Australia.
Email: shirlene@nadacaustralia.com
Web: www.nadacaustralia.com/

**Australian Flyball Association**
PO Box 4179, Pitt Town, NSW 2756
Tel: 0407 337 939
Email: info@flyball.org.au
Web: www.flyball.org.au/

*INTERNATIONAL*

**World Canine Freestyle Organisation**
P.O. Box 350122, Brooklyn, NY 11235-2525, USA
Tel: (718) 332-8336
Fax: (718) 646-2686
Email: wcfodogs@aol.com
Web: www.worldcaninefreestyle.org

## HEALTH

*UK*
**Alternative Veterinary Medicine Centre**
Chinham House, Stanford in the Vale, Oxfordshire, SN7 8NQ
Tel: 01367 710324
Fax: 01367 718243
Web: www.alternativevet.org/

**British Small Animal Veterinary Association**
Woodrow House, 1 Telford Way,
Waterwells Business Park, Quedgeley,
Gloucestershire, GL2 2AB
Tel: 01452 726700
Fax: 01452 726701
Email: customerservices@bsava.com
Web: http://www.bsava.com/

**Royal College of Veterinary Surgeons**
Belgravia House, 62-64 Horseferry Road,
London, SW1P 2AF
Tel: 0207 222 2001
Fax: 0207 222 2004
Email: admin@rcvs.org.uk
Web: www.rcvs.org.uk

*USA*
**American Holistic Veterinary Medical Association**
2218 Old Emmorton Road
Bel Air, MD 21015
Tel: 410 569 0795
Fax 410 569 2346
Email: office@ahvma.org
Web: www.ahvma.org/

**American Veterinary Medical Association**
1931 North Meacham Road, Suite 100,
Schaumburg, IL 60173-4360, USA.
Tel: 800 248 2862
Fax: 847 925 1329
Web: www.avma.org

**American College of Veterinary Surgeons**
19785 Crystal Rock Dr, Suite 305
Germantown, MD 20874, USA.
Tel: 301 916 0200
Toll Free: 877 217 2287
Fax: 301 916 2287
Email: acvs@acvs.org
Web: www.acvs.org/

*AUSTRALIA*
**Australian Holistic Vets**
Web: www.ahv.com.au/

**Australian Small Animal Veterinary Association**
40/6 Herbert Street, St Leonards, NSW 2065, Australia.
Tel: 02 9431 5090
Fax: 02 9437 9068
Email: asava@ava.com.au
Web: www.asava.com.au

**Australian Veterinary Association**
Unit 40, 6 Herbert Street, St Leonards, NSW 2065, Australia.
Tel: 02 9431 5000
Fax: 02 9437 9068
Web: www.ava.com.au

**Australian College Veterinary Scientists**
Building 3, Garden City Office Park,
2404 Logan Road, Eight Mile Plains,
Queensland 4113, Australia.
Tel: 07 3423 2016
Fax: 07 3423 2977
Email: admin@acvs.org.au
Web: http://acvsc.org.au

## ASSISTANCE DOGS

*UK*
**Canine Partners**
Mill Lane, Heyshott, Midhurst, GU29 0ED
Tel: 08456 580480
Fax: 08456 580481
Web: www.caninepartners.co.uk

**Dogs for the Disabled**
The Frances Hay Centre, Blacklocks Hill,
Banbury, Oxon, OX17 2BS
Tel: 01295 252600
Web: www.dogsforthedisabled.org

**Guide Dogs for the Blind Association**
Burghfield Common, Reading, RG7 3YG
Tel: 01189 835555
Fax: 01189 835433
Web: www.guidedogs.org.uk/

**Hearing Dogs for Deaf People**
The Grange, Wycombe Road, Saunderton,
Princes Risborough, Bucks, HP27 9NS
Tel: 01844 348100
Fax: 01844 348101
Web: www.hearingdogs.org.uk

**Pets as Therapy**
14a High Street, Wendover, Aylesbury, Bucks.
HP22 6EA.
Tel: 01845 345445
Fax: 01845 550236
Web: http://www.petsastherapy.org/

**Support Dogs**
21 Jessops Riverside, Brightside Lane, Sheffield, S9 2RX
Tel: 01142 617800
Fax: 01142 617555
Email: supportdogs@btconnect.com
Web: www.support-dogs.org.uk

*USA*
**Therapy Dogs International**
88 Bartley Road, Flanders, NJ 07836,.
Tel: 973 252 9800
Fax: 973 252 7171
Web: www.tdi-dog.o

**Therapy Dogs Inc.**
P.O. Box 20227, Cheyenne, WY 82003.
Tel: 307 432 0272.
Fax: 307-638-2079
Web: www.therapydogs.com

**Delta Society - Pet Partners**
875 124th Ave NE, Suite 101, Bellevue, WA 98005 USA.
Email: info@DeltaSociety.org
Web: www.deltasociety.org

**Comfort Caring Canines**
8135 Lare Street, Philadelphia, PA 19128.
Email: ccc@comfortcaringcanines.org
Web: www.comfortcaringcanines.org/

*AUSTRALIA*
**AWARE Dogs Australia, Inc**
PO Box 883, Kuranda, Queensland, 488..
Tel: 07 4093 8152
Web: www.awaredogs.org.au/

**Delta Society — Therapy Dogs**
Web: www.deltasociety.com.au